A LEAGUE *of* YOUR OWN

Leadership Lessons with All-Star Athletes Who Want **YOU** to **WIN** in Sports, School and Life!

JENN STARKEY & THE LEGACY LEAGUE

Starkey, Jenn

A League Of Your Own: Leadership Lessons with All-Star Athletes Who Want You to Win in Sports, School and Life!

Impact Project 2015: 2nd Edition Print

ISBN-13: 978-0-692-45801-3

GO ONLINE FOR AN INTERACTIVE EDITION OF THIS BOOK AT

WWW.LOYOBOOK.COM

THIS BOOK IS AVAILABLE AT SPECIAL QUANITY DISCOUNTS TO USE FOR EDUCATIONAL TRAINING PROGRAMS. FOR MORE INFORMATION, PLEASE CONTACT THE PUBLISHER AT **Impact@LoyoBook.com**.

MVP IMPACT PROJECT 2015

For those who desire to make an impact.

Table of Contents

✪ IMPACT

✪ SPIRIT- Bonus Chapters

THE PREGAME

Do you have big dreams? One of my coaches once told me "If you have a dream, first you must build a team!" I learned the hard way; this statement is only *partially true*. From earning a softball scholarship to my dream school to watch my life turn upside down, I discovered it takes much more than "the dream team" to be successful. If you want to win in sports, school and life you have to play in *a league of your own.*

A league is a group of people who work together for a common mission. **When you find a league of your own, life is better in every way.** Imagine feeling confident and strong, constantly surrounded by people who believe in you and value your gifts. What would it be like to be surrounded by a team that inspires you everyday? How would you feel if you *knew* you had a team that just 'gets you'; that will pick you up when you are down and celebrate with you when you succeed? We call this team your *POWER TEAM.*

This book is **your game plan** for how to live *The League of Your Own* lifestyle. As you read this book, you will discover how to find the team, the tools and the toughness to overcome any obstacle. You'll reach your dreams faster, while having more fun!

ALL-STAR LEADERSHIP QUIZ

HINT: Answer YES to the following questions

1. Do you want to be successful?
2. Do you want meaningful friendships?
3. Do you want to be healthy and athletic?
4. Do you want to feel confident and energized?
5. Do you want to become wealthy or financially free while doing work you love?
6. Do you want to make a positive impact in the world, while having a ton of fun?
7. *Are you still reading this right now?*

Did you say yes to one or more of the previous questions?

YES?... WHEW!...Good! You passed the quiz!

Congratulations! You have been accepted into the official all-star leadership initiation process.

You're now ready to continue...

Take the full leadership quiz online now
www.Loyobook.com/guide

NEVER SKIP THE WARM-UP

Wooooooo- Hoooooo!

You MADE IT! You found the secret initiation to our exclusive MVP All-Star club. Over the next few pages you'll discover if you have what it takes to join our club of athletes who are literally changing the world!

Can you feel the electricity of this book in your hands? *HINT: On a scale of 1 to 10 on the excited scale. Jump up and down, 10 times, yell out a big "WOO- HOO" at the top of your lungs and try again... you'll feel it. You might as well start celebrating now, because **this book is going to change your life.***

"Woah, woah, woah!" I know what you're thinking. "I don't even know you! How will a book change anything? How can a book help me get my homework done or move up to the top of the lineup? You don't even know me!" Sigh, It's true, you might not know me yet, I might not know you yet, but we will take care of that momentarily.

This book is for leaders. Leaders are action takers. If you are an action taker, then you might as well start celebrating now, because **this book will show you how to WIN in school, sports and life!**

1. FUNDAMENTALS OF SUCCESS

Have you ever wondered if you are smart enough, fast enough, strong enough, tall enough, pretty enough or good enough to deserve greatness in your life? **How do you know if you have what it takes?** Do you have *the fuel, the focus and the fire* it takes to make it to the top?

Truth bomb #1

(Insert exploding sound effect here for dramatic effect.)

You are it! The only person preventing you from having everything in life you have ever dreamed of is you. **Everything you need to enjoy success in your life is already within you!** You already have what it takes! I know it, the rest of the authors in this book know it; the question is... Do you?

You are not alone!

My name is Coach Jenn. You can find my picture on the back of this book; along with the other coaches I will introduce to you soon. Together, we are here to **help you discover your inner strength** and guide you through challenges you may face on your journey to reach your goals in sports, school and life.

We all face different challenges at different points in our journey. Maybe you are having trouble in your relationships and people you know have been giving you a hard time for one reason or another. Perhaps you have been feeling overwhelmed with responsibility and you are trying to figure out how to balance school, with homework and some kind of social life. Maybe you aren't feeling good in your own body, you're at war with those negative voices in your own head and it's hard to see how things could ever change.

Whatever you may be today, I've brought together this elite team of coaches and mentors who will help you tackle your obstacles. Remember no matter where you are or what you are facing, **you are never alone. There is an entire team of people out there cheering for you, even if you can't hear us!** You can accomplish far more than you may believe you are capable of.

Trust the Process

Now you might be thinking. "OH! COME ON! I know I have what it takes! My life is pretty sweet. I don't care about all of this personality quizzing, "Rah—Rah" hoopla! Just get to the meat! I want results! I want them now! Teach me how to run faster so I can steal more bases, or how to get noticed so I can make the varsity team… or earn a scholarship!"

If this is you, pay attention. I get you. I am just like you. From this point on, I will affectionately call you *Turbo*. Do your best to channel your inner monk. (Take a deep breath in... and out... OM. Chant with me, "OM.")

We are going to share what it takes to become a great athlete and a great leader that coaches want on their team. With that said, just like in sports, we start with the fundamentals and the basics of what it takes to win!

The first step to becoming successful is to feel that deep burning desire to create, to experience or become something. It is obviously clear you have the desire because you are still reading! You have already made over half way through the introduction; I am ceremoniously awarding you 10 MVP points! Yay! You can redeem them at the end of the book for fun prizes!

Truth bomb #2

(Insert multiple exploding sound effects here, for an enhanced dramatic effect.) **Showing up is not enough.** Being a good person and a hard worker isn't enough for you to reach your dreams. Just because you are a star pitcher on your softball team doesn't mean you'll earn a scholarship to college. Just because you go to college doesn't mean you get a great job. And, just because you get a great job, doesn't mean you'll be happy or financially independent. However, if you take action and follow the game plan in this book, you will have the tools to be prepared for many things life could throw your way!

My commitment to you

I am your sherpa, your guide, your coach, I am on your team! We are on this journey together. This book is your vehicle. *Please keep your arms and legs inside the vehicle at all times.* Each chapter marks a path from where you are, to where you want to be! Think of it like we are going on a road trip together. WOO-HOO, road trip with Coach Jenn and the first thing we do on a road trip is set our GPS!

No matter where you are today, if you are willing to trust the process, this book will provide more insight than you can possibly imagine. In fact, this book is filled with so much life changing information, I've considered taking out a readers' insurance policy, just in case your head actually explodes. (Your family probably wouldn't be very happy with me if that were to happen. They love you and they have entrusted me with your care, so we are going to cover the ground rules first!)

The playing field

The world we live in is uncharted territory. In many ways it is like we are heading towards a modern day *'wild, wild west.'* The skills we need to be successful in our world are different from the skills our grandparents needed. We can't rely on school to give us the tools we need for success, happiness and fulfillment.

Our parents need help too! Our world is so different from the one they grew up in; it's hard for them to know how to prepare us for everything. As young a leader, if you want to make an impact in your life and others, **you must take matters into your own hands.**

...I come bearing good news!

Because you were born into this exact moment in time, **you have the opportunity to have a bigger impact on the course of human history than any other generation, ever!** Take a deep breath! It's no pressure. Really. Here you thought you were reading a book about sports and BAM! *Surprise!* You find yourself reading a guide to saving the world!

Yes, we're going to set you up to win in sports and we're also giving you the secrets to win in life. As much as you love to play softball, there is MUCH more to who you are. **You have many gifts to offer** this world!

Who will win?

There is an old saying "The secret to success is not about *what* you know, it's about *who* you know." I believe there is more to this secret. I believe success isn't just who you know, but more importantly who you choose to believe in, and *who believes in you!*

In our new world, there are no limitations to the people you can connect with and learn from! Our new world will be defined by the people who understand how to build and nurture relationships, people who learn to inspire others to work together for a common mission. Our new world will be designed by the people who take their education into their own hands and let nothing stand in their way from reaching their goals.

By making the commitment to surround yourself with successful people who believe in you, you can **jump** straight to the big leagues of life. Our new world will be led by you!

A word of caution...

There are people in life who will challenge the ideas presented in this book. They may not understand your new habits or goals. I have met many people who don't understand the big picture just yet. That is okay. Just remember, the people willing to sacrifice integrity for trophies, ruin relationships for the spotlight and ignore expert advice for the convenient path, will eventually struggle. *I learned some of this the hard way, but you don't have to.*

As mentors, we will share our experiences with you, our successes and struggles. We keep it real and we will give you tools you can use to make your life easier. **Focus on just one or two things** from each coach that make you feel your best.

Your time is now!

In this book, you'll meet the team I wish I had when I was in your shoes. I'm honored to introduce you to them. They have taught me so much about what it means to be a leader and I know you will love learning from them too. We are on your power team and **we believe in you.**

2. THE LOYO LIFE

The LOYOlife is awesome. When you live the league of your own lifestyle, (LOYOlife for short) it means you can enjoy a life of full of success, freedom & significance. It is simple to live the LOYOlife, but just because it is simple does not mean it is always easy. Sometimes we are faced with challenges that test our commitment and other times, without even knowing it, we sabotage ourselves.

Have you ever set a huge goal, something that seems like it would be the ultimate accomplishment? Only when you finally reach the goal, you don't feel successful after all? All the sudden it's "No. Big. Deal."

I used to struggle with this. "Perfectionist" was my middle name. I claimed the name like a badge of honor. Like most driven athletes, I would set a goal, but as soon as I reached it, it seemed like it wasn't as cool anymore. I had this attitude, this belief I could have and should have done better. My perfectionism meant I always felt this sense of dissatisfaction with myself. That dissatisfaction grew into doubt. That doubt started eating at my confidence. At one point, I wouldn't even try something unless I KNEW I could win and be successful at it. I now know perfection is a monster excuse disguised as our friend. If you let it, perfectionism will slowly eat away at your dreams and goals until one day it begins to eat away at your spirit.

I didn't think I was worthy of being part of a team! My "perfectionist" issue was preventing me from reaching my goals, from living life with purpose and becoming a person of impact. I started believing I couldn't help others, unless I reached a certain level of "success" myself. **That was one of the greatest lies I ever believed.** Perfection is not the goal of the LOYOlife.

Identify your goal – Listen to the Whisper

Can you imagine playing a softball game with out any bases, or a basketball game with out any baskets? We know if you want to win a game, we have to have a goal. Most people say "they want to be successful" but they don't know where the goals are. That is kind of like saying "I want to win the game" with out knowing how to score a point.

In life, we get to set our own goals. With out a goal, we just end up running around with out any way to know if we are getting any better. But how do we know what our goals should be? What is a worthy goal anyway?

In middle school, I went to a pitcher/catcher camp at a local university. I went to work on my catching skills. When I got there, there were a ton of catchers, but only a few pitchers. It was like this little tickly whisper said, "try pitching!" So I did. That tickle turned into this itchy feeling

10

that I needed to become the person who could help my team in any situation. As you can imagine, there were many coaches who told me I should just pick one. You can't be a pitcher AND a catcher. But *I still had this desire* to learn both!

The night before I began high school, it took *forever* to fall asleep. My goal was to make the varsity softball team. Surely, that would be the stamp of approval saying, *"I was good enough."*

I stared at the ceiling, playing a movie in my head. I saw myself heading to practice, impressing the coach with my laser arm, running faster in my mind than my feet could probably move in real life.

I didn't make varsity that year. I caught every game for the JV team. I had fun and I didn't reach my goal. Sometimes the movie doesn't play out exactly how we see it in our head.

Success comes quietly

Sophomore year I made varsity as an outfielder. A few games into pre-season, our senior pitcher got into big trouble. She made a choice to go to a party. There was alcohol at the party. Our coach didn't care if she drank or not, her choice to go to this party where people were drinking resulted in her suspension for the majority of our season. I became a starting varsity pitcher "overnight."

I thought *I didn't earn this... I only received an opportunity because someone else made a mistake.* It was hard to understand that even though someone else's mistake gave me an opportunity, it was my hard work, my choices and daily preparation leading up to that day, that put me in the position to succeed. **I had reached my goal** to help my team in any situation and I didn't even recognize it.

As an athlete and leader, *success is a habit*. There is no cheer squad with glitter hats and streamers when we make the daily choices that move us closer to our goals. Success is built, brick by brick, with the small daily choices we make that move us closer to our goal. **If we are only focusing on the destination, we miss out on magical moments that make our journey special.**

Celebrate where you are today

Today, my life is pretty amazing. I'm writing this book, I am strong in my faith, I have great relationships with my family and I recently got married to my very best friend! I'm thankful for my health, my supportive friendships with people who inspire me, and the chance to make a positive impact in the world doing what I love!

I share this with you because I am so very proud of what I have accomplished, and I want you to be proud of what you accomplish too! **This is what success really looks like;** finding joy in your daily habits and pride in your personal growth.

Have I been perfect? No WAY! Neither will you, nor will anyone else who pursues excellence. But **you deserve to have pride,** not in one of those "big headed" or "cocky attitude" kinds of ways, but in a way that honors your effort and the many people who support you in your journey.

It's like Crossfit for your soul.

To me, pride means having personal satisfaction when overcoming adversity. YOU WILL have adversity and challenges in your life and **you can overcome them.** It's like lifting weights. In order to build muscle you have to put your body under stress. **When it comes building strength in character, your mind will be put under stress too.** On the other side of adversity and stress, you have the opportunity to grow stronger than you can imagine!

When I was 13, I had two big goals. The first was to have my own business making movies that would *change the world*. The second was to go to a school where I could learn filmmaking, play Division 1 softball and help my team earn a chance to compete in the Women's College World Series. Again, the movie in my mind did NOT play out how it had debuted in my head.

*Important Notice!

This story has a happy ending but it doesn't start out that way. I am going to share with you one very personal, difficult experience. You or someone you know may have experienced something similar, or not. Stay with me and **we will make it to the other side, stronger together.**

My crossroad

I DID earn a scholarship to the SCHOOL of my dreams! It was in New York City! There I could learn to make movies and play Division 1 softball. IT WAS AMAZING!

You could see the empire state building beyond left field and we ran back and fourth across the Brooklyn Bridge for our early morning workouts. I loved the independence that came from being away from my Texas home. I believed the popular New York saying *"If you could make it here... you can make it anywhere."*

It was about a week before our spring season began. My teammates were going out for a birthday celebration. There would be drinking. I decided to stay at the dorms, as I usually did. I wasn't anti-social, but I was really focused on what was important to me. I felt better when I had a good night's sleep and I tried to fit in extra workouts outs when I could.

This night was different. It was the end of February and cold outside. I was feeling frustrated with myself. I didn't feel like I was fitting in. I didn't understand my role on the team. I was going to class and doing extra work. Some of my teammates were not even going to class. It didn't seem fair. I wanted to have fun like everyone else!

I decided to take a break from my papers and go down to play video games with some friends on the boys' floor. There was alcohol there as well, many different colored bottles, plastic cups and a room of people who looked like they were having a good time.

I never drank in high school; and I never felt like I was missing out either. We had fun with out it. In college, it seemed like it was everywhere. It even seemed that was the primary way people had fun and made friends. In high school, I had *a league of my own*; we had built habits that helped us reach our goals, alcohol wasn't part of our culture. I hadn't built that group of friends in college yet.

While my teammates were out drinking in the city, I thought it wouldn't be a big deal to drink in the dorms. I had an early practice, but as long as I didn't drink very much, I thought I would be okay. I would have one night of relaxation and fun, one night to be like everyone else and get back to my training schedule as usual. **I was wrong.**

Someone I knew gave me a drink, an athlete I trusted. I drank it. Later that night I was sexually assaulted and raped in the dorms.

The toughest call

It was daylight. Chunks of my memory were missing. At first, I thought I had done something wrong. I needed to get dressed for practice but I couldn't move.

My friends led me to the supervisors of the dorms but they weren't properly educated on what to do. I went to the hospital alone. My mom called when I was there. I hesitated to pick up the phone.

"Hi Mom."

"Hey Jenn, I just wanted to check in on you. I hadn't heard from you in a while. How are you?"

"I'm fine, umm...just tired." I cried in silence. I couldn't tell her. She was half way across the country and I was scared. I thought I would disappoint her. I didn't want to make her sad, or mad!

When I made the decision to go to the police and file a report, the first person I met laughed at me. After finally finding someone that would listen to me, they handed me over to an official New York City detective. I rode from one old building to another in the back of a NYPD police car. Looking out the window, I thought how very different this was from the rides to softball practice in Texas where I grew up.

Later, the detective brought me into a small closet-like room stacked floor to ceiling with manila folders. The room smelled old. He asked me a couple quick questions before telling me that I was lying. He said I should be ashamed of my actions; I should keep my mouth shut and move on with my life.

It's a very scary position to be in when the people who are we're told are supposed to protect us and take care of you aren't there for you.

That led to the toughest all I've ever made in my entire life. I don't know if days or weeks had gone by. I found an empty office in the corner of the building, hid under a desk and dialed home.

Very quickly after that call, my parents helped me decide it would be best if I came home. I had dedicated so much of my life to the dream of playing college softball, it seemed everything I had worked for was gone, almost overnight. Earning a scholarship to the school of my dreams became another accomplishment I could no longer claim to be proud of. While my team was kicking-off the **best season ever** together, I was flying home for my worst.

The worst part wasn't what happened to me, or the fact that I gave up my scholarship. The worst part was I had lost my team, all my friends and my own identity in the process. Any shred of confidence I might have had was gone. For a very long time, I felt completely alone.

Don't you worry... Don't you worry, child.

I am not sharing this with you to get you down. This story ends up with a very happy ending! This is just a story, of someone like you who overcame adversity and got stronger in the process. Sometimes things happen we don't understand, things that make no sense in the moment. This is my story, but it isn't uncommon. Every day I am reminded of many kinds of hard roads we all face at different points in our life.

Some of us have to deal with horrific bullying, for others it's divorce of our parents. Some of us lose loved ones. Sometimes we just don't make the team, no matter how hard we try. Often it's a combination of these things that stack on top of each other, until it seems like we just can't take any

17

more. That is moment you find out you are stronger than you thought you were!

There are still moments when I get mad or sad however if I had the opportunity to back in time, I wouldn't change anything. My experience in life has given me a perspective that allows me to serve others in a unique way. Just like your story gives you a unique power to make a difference in the world that only you can make! *It is often our greatest challenge that leads to our greatest growth and success!*

This book isn't about MY story... it's about yours!

We want to protect you, prepare you and propel you!

Some people get uncomfortable when I share my story. I think that may be because they don't know how to respond, or maybe they are not yet comfortable with experiences they have had in their own life. This is okay. I share my story because I want you to know, whatever you may be facing now or in the future, you aren't alone.

Sometimes things happen that are out of your control, you deserve to know that you are not any less worthy of celebrating your victories when they do. Your past doesn't define you. No matter how big the challenges you have faced in your past may seem, or what may come in your future, *you will always be okay*. You get to choose the meaning of your story. Which means your story *will* have a happy ending too! In the mean time, it's okay to celebrate the journey and exactly where you are today!

The puzzle

No matter how horrible or difficult a situation may be, there is always something positive that can be gained from it, something you can learn from, something that helps you grow. This can take time, but it's possible! When you get to a place and time when you can accept all of your experiences, positive or negative, have built you into the person you are today, you will see everything in your life will start to fit together like a perfectly designed puzzle. I call this *The Play Up Puzzle*!

I believe, when you are born, you are given a small pile of puzzle pieces. When you look at your pieces they don't all fit together right away. **Your pieces are made of your talents, your desires, your relationships and your experiences.**

When you have a random desire like "I really want to be a pitcher AND a catcher" or a tough experience that doesn't make any sense, you might not see how these pieces are supposed to fit. That is because you don't know what the big picture, the finished puzzle, looks like yet. As you move forward in life, you start to meet people with the other puzzle pieces you need. **Your job in life** is to stand up and proudly say, "HEY, I don't know what this whole puzzle looks like yet, but here is what I do know! Here are the experiences I've had, maybe they can help you out too!" The more often you "Play Up", or surround yourself with others who think positively and believe in you, the more clear the picture will become!

The platform

After I came home from New York, I had the opportunity to go and play for my second dream school. *So LUCKY!!!* I KNOW.

At my first school I was recruited as a catcher, so guess what position I played at my second school?... That's right! I was recruited as a pitcher! (Can I get a "Boo-Yah!!!") After being out of school for over 10 months and then returning back to the classroom, I saw things differently. While I LOVED school, it was easy to see how **even the top universities in the world aren't able to keep up** with the changes happening in the world.

I had learned that I couldn't rely on my teachers to give me all of the tools I needed to be successful. I needed to take responsibility for my education and my success.

We went to nationals and then I left that school after just one season. It was 2009, and both of my parents had lost their jobs with in a week of each other. Even though I could have gone to school for basically free, it made more sense *for me* to help support my family and go all in towards my dreams by starting a business! The pressure was on!

The process

Here is the cool thing about winning in sports and life; if you can figure out how you were successful in one area of your life, you can often use the same formula, apply it to something new to become successful there too!

Step 1: find a great coach

I quickly learned if I was going to be halfway decent in business, I would need to find a coach, just like to be successful in the game of softball we look for a great hitting or pitching coach. If you have big goals, a mentor can help guide you on your journey and shorten the learning curve.

After working with a mentor, I started to see some quick success! However, there was still something missing. I was making money, but I wasn't really happy. I was trying to figure out how to fit my puzzle pieces of desires, talents, skills and experiences together. As I tried to force pieces together, I DID NOT always listen to my mentor. I kept messing up and making mistakes. Two steps forward, a dozen steps back. My coach got me started down the right path but there was more to success than finding a great coach.

Step 2: Learn the tools and practice them

The voices in my head were getting louder. I was struggling in my relationships, with my family, financially. I started to blame my past. I started to become a victim instead of the creator of my own story.

The voices followed me everywhere, screaming: "You never finish anything! You have never accomplished anything! No one cares about you! Who are you to be a leader? What difference can you make? Who is going to listen to you?" I was drowning. I might have stayed stuck there forever; instead one of my mentors taught me **a secret weapons to fight the voices that were tearing me down.**

Ask better questions. All of the voices in our heads are actually answering questions we are asking ourselves. For example, if I asked: *"Why do I feel so lonely?"* The mean voice would respond with echoes of the detective "You are a horrible person!" This was not helping me live the life I wanted. So instead I had to practice asking better questions. Questions like: "What could I get excited about in my life now?" and "If I could be thankful for something today, what could I be thankful for?"

Our brains are like Google. If we ask a bad question, we will get an equally bad answer. But if we ask a more empowering question, our brains are capable of giving us more helpful answers. *"What was the #1 thing that helped me to become a successful athlete?"* This was the most revealing question yet.

Step 3: The Play Up Principle

Have you ever 'played up'? Have you ever practiced or played with bigger, older and stronger players in the sports you love? I remembered when I played softball; I would "Play Up" as often as I could with older teams. I wanted to play with athletes that would challenge me! Having a great coach was only part of the puzzle. Practicing with tools took me another step closer.... But the Play Up Principle is the secret sauce that allows average people to live extraordinary lives.

If you are committed to living the extraordinary league of your own lifestyle, we need to be part of a team of bigger, older, "stronger" players who challenge us to become better. I became 100% committed to building my power team. This is where the biggest shift can happen for you!

Putting it all together

Every talent, desire, relationship and experience you have ever had, creates a grand puzzle that reveals your purpose on earth. Throughout this book, you'll get to meet several of my mentors and you'll also get to know a few young all-stars I've had the opportunity to personally mentor along the way, as part of MVP Leadership Academy. As you read their success stories you'll begin to realize how each of the pieces of the all-star leadership puzzle can begin working as a vehicle in your life, no matter where your destination may be.

You can't win the game alone, and the great thing is you don't have to. There is a team of people in the palm of your hand who can help you put together your puzzle.

3. THE BIG PICTURE

Truth bomb #3

(Cue exploding sound effect with extra bass this time.)

You are either ALL IN, or you are out. All-Star leaders want to invest their time with other all-star leaders. If you are not willing to commit to the league of your own lifestyle, you won't find yourself in the club for very long.

WAIT, STOP! I know that voice that popped up in your head is saying "But wait, Coach Jenn! I thought you said your power team was made of super successful people? I want to be successful, but what can I possibly bring to the table that is worthy enough to deserve such an amazing power team?" To you I say *"SHUSHHHH!"*

You are already MORE than worthy of all of the love, support and advice any one of our Legacy Leaguers could ever provide. If you are willing to **dig deep daily** in pursuit of your dreams, we will be there to cheer you on and support you.

7 myths about leadership and success!

To help you build that undeniable self-belief, let's debunk seven myths about leadership that may currently be holding you back from your potential.

1. You don't need all of the steps to get started.

While having a vision of the future is important, you don't have to see or know every step in order to get started. Do you think when Steve Jobs first launched Apple he knew exactly how he would build the iPhone and launch the app store and transform the world as we know it. NO WAY, Jose! He was working out of a garage, barefooted. (Probably still wearing the same black turtleneck he wore for his entire life.) Great leaders don't have to know *how* to do everything. They just need to understand *WHY* they are committed to doing it.

Steve jobs built apple to help people create things with more ease. I got my first Apple computer at age 14. It changed my life. I was able to edit videos. Publish my first blog and make my first podcast. If it wasn't for Steve, I don't believe you would be reading this book. Steve didn't build apple by himself. He surrounded himself with other great people and asked great questions!

When I first had the idea of MVP Leadership academy, I was living in a one-bedroom apartment. I had been working all the time on building a business I didn't REALLY love. I was exhausted and unhappy.

I woke up in the middle of the night and felt a very strong *desire* to go write. I filled up an entire spiral notebook that night. Every page filled with questions. These questions seemed to flow through me like my fingers were writing on their own. They wrote the following words:

Build a Team, Write a Book, Grow youth sports around the world.

I had NO IDEA how I was going to do any of that Obviously we are still on this journey so we will see how it all shakes out.

The next day I launched a Facebook page called **Fastpitch Fit.** I started reaching out and asking new fans TONS of questions. I asked about their challenges and their desires and did my best to help them when I could. I made videos, ran contests and posted pictures for two years without ever selling anything. I focused on building a community, and got in touch with what people needed, sometimes questioning why I was investing so much time, energy and money this way.

In the process of working towards this goal I have stumbled MANY, MANY times. I let down complete strangers because I made promises to deliver things before I had the resources. Like in the daydream before my freshmen year, my mind was running faster than my feet could, but I never lost site of the mission and why it was important to keep moving forward. You have to have faith things will work out. I knew eventually I would make it up to those people who supported me along the way.

Fast-forward to now, I would say things are coming together quite nicely. Of course, our first book is now done, and MVP Leadership academy is already making an impact around the world!

2. You don't have to be 'Miss Popularity' to make an impact.

You don't have to be popular to be a leader, but you might become popular because you are a leader. If that is not your goal, of course you don't have to be front and center! Many of our greatest leaders you have probably never heard of!

A woman named Beate Sirota Gordan, was a 22 year old American, who went on a journey to Japan to find her parents after World War II. Her personal puzzle pieces led her to single-handedly write women's rights into the constitution of modern Japan. She kept this a secret for many decades! She was a 22 year-old immigrant "no body" who led an entire population of people to enjoy the freedoms we enjoy here in the USA. She has definitely made an impact on the world we live in today!

3. You don't have to always feel happy or positive to be a leader.

The way you feel isn't always reflective of who you are. As you learn to master your emotions you'll start to think of each emotion as a messenger. Some you listen to and those that don't serve you, you can learn to ignore.

Okay Turbo, I know you are thinking "BUT COACH JENN! I'M A TEENAGE GIRL! Do you know what happens to teenage girls? I have these crazy mood swings and they happen... like at least once every month, and sometimes it feels like every day!"

Oh, I KNOW!! I experience mood swings that some times feel like I have amnesia, and will never feel 'normal again.' But you always do, and there are things you can do to help with this! *(If there are any boys reading this, don't bail! You have come this far and I promise reading this book to the end will give you an edge no other young man has in MANY areas of your life.)*

Great leaders learn to be aware of their emotions and use them as tools. They then learn how and when to tune them out. You can actually change your emotions from negative to positive instantly. No matter how bad you may feel. This is a skill that can be learned! It just takes a little information and practice!

4. You don't have to have the perfect body or perfect health for people to follow you.

This is a big one! Being healthy and strong is important to have the energy you need to dig deep towards your goals. Health is a daily habit and is critical to success. Having the *perfect body*, or the perfect health is NOT a prerequisite for being a leader.

29

You may have heard the story of Lauren Hill. She was diagnosed with an inoperable brain tumor. During the last 18 months of her life, Lauren was able to not only fulfill her own personal dream of playing college basketball, but she was able to raise well over $1,000,000 for cancer research to fight this life-threatening disease. She used the platform of basketball to make a difference in millions of lives. Lauren passed away in April of 2015, but the Impact she has made in this world will not soon be forgotten.

I never got to meet Lauren, but she represents everything it means to be part of the Legacy League. Later, you will hear from another author, who in elementary school was able to lead her team even when she was in and out of the hospital every day.

5. You don't have to start out super rich to have expert mentors.

When people see greatness in you, they want to invest in you because they want to be part of your success story! Most of the Legacy Leaguers involved in the MVP Leadership Academy Programs share simply because they see greatness in you! They believe in our mission to help you succeed in sports, school and life and they want to give back! This enables you to get access to elite level training as part of our MVP All-Star Club every month for less than most weekly hitting lessons cost!

Plus, you can start learning from expert mentors for free by tuning into podcasts, checking out books from the library and asking great questions of people you respect! You can start learning success principles no matter how much money you currently have personally.

6. It doesn't matter how old you are.
As you read this book, you will see stories from girls as young as 10 years old making a difference in their lives and the lives of others. But we will save those stories for later. It is never too early or too late to "play up."

7. Luck has little to do with it.
When you become super successful, you will hear comments like "Oh my gosh, how did you get so lucky?" Secret: "Lucky people" get lucky because they have they never give up. "Lucky people" get lucky because when an opportunity to grow falls in their lap, and they go all in without hesitation, with confidence. "Lucky people" prepare, are patient and put themselves in a position to succeed at all times. They understand every day and every opportunity is a gift. "Lucky people" are committed and "lucky people" believe there is always something good headed their way! You can create your own luck!

7 Pieces All-Star Leadership

Before we can lead others, we must first build enough strength to lead our own lives. The stories and activities in the remainder of this book will help you build a strong foundation in each principal pieces of the all-star leadership puzzle.

The book is broken up into 7 sections, just like 7 innings of a softball game. You need to win in each section, in order to win the ultimate game of life. Each *section* you will meet two coaches that will give you the tools and strategies to create your very own league of your own lifestyle.

1. **Vision:** Learn how to deal with naysayers, share your vision, and lead your team!

2. **Relationships:** Create a plan for being the best teammate in all situations and brand yourself so coaches want to recruit you!

3. **Emotions:** Learn a tool to master your emotions bust through challenges from holding you back!

4. **Health:** You will learn how to prevent injury, become faster and become more athletic!

5. **Career:** Get ahead of the competition by investing in yourself and find out if you are on the right career path for you.

6. **Impact:** Find out how to follow your dreams, build a great life and make a difference in the world by leading others.

7. **Spirit:** Learn how 3-time Olympic gold medalist and Former Team USA uses Faith as a source of personal strength both on and off the field.

You cannot become an All-Star leader until you have an understanding of the big picture and how your puzzle pieces begin to fit together.

BONUS! At the end of each section, you will find a story from one of our MVP all-stars. All-Star Club is a power team of girls just like you! We value sports and we are on a mission to make an impact helping others! These all-stars, ages 10-17 will share how their personal all-star club experience is helping them live the #LOYOLife and how you can too!

ALL STAR IN ACTION

Now it time for your FIRST #LOYOLife Activity.
DOWNLOAD the entire action guide at
www.LoyoBook.com/guide and print it out at home!

Yes, you can write in the book!

Let's practice first by writing your name and date:

_____

NAME

_____

DATE

If you have never written in a book before, feel free to give it a try and see what happens. You might like it. If anyone gives you a hard time about writing in a book, you can have him or her email me at Impact@LOYOBOOK.com
Disclaimer, do not write in library books, borrowed books, books you have yet to purchase from the store, or any books you might find sitting on your parents antique & collectible book shelf. That would be bad news.

35

Time to Play Up

Great Job! I know you are committed to becoming the best leader you can possibly be, in sports in school and in life. Feel free to underline or highlight any "Ah-Ha" moments you discover in each chapter. **You can even make little notes of questions you may want to one day ask a mentor on a live training call!** As you have fun getting to know each coach, consider how their stories may relate to experiences in your own life!

When you find something in this book you really love, start sharing today! Highlight a sentence and post a pic on Instagram. Tweet your favorite quote, or buy a copy of the book for a friend. Use #LOYOLife on social media to have a conversation with our coaches and with other girls like you! It is time to *Play Up*!

All-Star
VISION
/ˈviZHən/ noun

1.   **The ability or state of being able to see.**

-   the ability to think about or plan the future
with imagination & wisdom.

-   a mental image of what the future will or
could be like.

synonyms: imagination, creativity, inventiveness,
innovation, inspiration, intuition, perception, insight.

What does All-Star Vision mean to you?

Submitted by

KATIE DEWEY, 16

When I think of All—Star Vision I am reminded of this quote: "We all go through rough times. We have obstacles that seem too large to overcome. We have to decide what matters most to us
— Our Passions."

✪ VISION

Your vision is your ability to see a mental image or picture of your future, like playing a movie in your head of what you want your world to look like. Understanding where you want to go and what you want your life to look like is your first step to putting together your personal play up puzzle.

Think of your vision, like setting the GPS in your car. It creates the map for your brain to take you where you want to go! If you don't take the time to set your GPS, it could take you much longer to get where you want to go, and you are more likely to get lost along the way.

In this section, you will meet two amazing women that will help you to get clear on your vision, and help you communicate that vision with your team.

Meet Coach Jill

Have you ever had a big dream so big that when you shares your goal with another person they told you it wouldn't happen?! They might have said things like: *You should be more realistic, or your chances are slim or even impossible!*

Jill Wolforth is not your average pitching instructor. In fact, elite athletes and coaches travel across the entire world to The Texas Baseball Ranch where she and her husband deliver their one-of-a-kind athletic training programs. The athletes they train live the **#LOYOlife.**

One of Jill's special gifts is the ability to find areas in your development that may be keeping you from reaching your potential.

Jill was an academic All-American and competed in two Women's College World Series while attending University of Nebraska.

In this chapter Jill shares:

- ✓ The **9 elements to athletic success** that most people forget.
- ✓ Top **tools to make your vision stronger** so you can be more successful.
- ✓ **3 ways to get unstuck** or out of a slump even when you feel like you have tried everything!

4. SET YOUR GPS

A Conversation with Coach Jill Wolforth...

At a recent mindset presentation with some of the professional players who train at the baseball ranch, we were talking about the importance of *clarity*. We played a video clip from motivational speaker Tony Robbins who discussed the importance of having the right map for what you're trying to obtain. Tony stated that it's one thing to be really excited and really motivated to get something accomplished but if you aren't clear on the path, you can have unlimited motivation and you will still fail.

His example was "running east looking for a sunset." He explained how you could be bound and determined to see the sunset, the only problem is you're running east and that's simply not going to work, because the sun sets in the west. **If you want to be successful, you need to have a map!** Maps tell you where to go, they include boundaries, obstacles and routes that make it possible for you to reach your destination.

You also need to constantly work at improving your map and gaining more clarity. If you look back over time at drawings of world maps, you'll see that it has certainly evolved. The first drawings, as well as subsequent drawings were based on what people believed the world looked like, based on the information they had at that time.

Here is Ptolemy's World Map (2ⁿᵈ century) in a 15th century reconstruction:

As time passed and tools progressed so did the maps. Here's an 18ᵗʰ century world map. Notice it says at the top A NEW AND CORRECT MAP of the WORLD".

And now today…

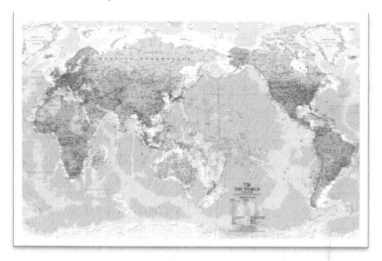

Look at how different the first map was different. Things became clearer over time, because overtime our measuring tools improved.   But even if you don't have the perfect tools, you must start somewhere. This is a key point. *Make your map for what you want and make it as clear as you can, based on what you know at the present moment.* You then continue to add details or clarity to the map as you learn more.

What are a few tools athletes can use to get a clearer picture of where they are today and where they need to go to reach their goals?

We are very fortunate today because we have so many tools that will help us add clarity. In softball, we can use video to analyze our own skills. Most smart phones come with a slow motion option so you can watch your form for running, hitting, throwing or pitching. You can use YouTube to learn from top coaches, athletes and teachers on almost any topic. You can use radar guns and stop watches to measure velocity improvement or speed improvement. You can also get help from specialists in nutrition, physical therapy, speed, recruiting or almost any area you need help with clarity.

Just remember, you can be extremely motivated to accomplish something, but you must be very clear about where you are today and map out the direction you must go in order to achieve it. Once you have your map, the only piece left is your willingness to do what it takes to go for it.

Why do you think some people with big goals, don't take the daily action required to reach it?

On a fairly regular basis at The Texas Baseball Ranch you will hear Coach Wolforth say, "Have a big enough 'why' and the 'how' will become self-evident". I think most people, don't get clear enough on their why's.

Roger Clemens was one of the most dominant pitchers in major league history, they nicknamed him 'The Rocket.' When Roger was growing up his mother worked a night shift, as a cleaning lady, scrubbing floors in order to provide for her family as a single mother. Roger tells the story of having this image imprinted in his mind. It was a major 'why' for him; he wanted to make a great living so that his mother NEVER had to work on her knees scrubbing floors again. That's a pretty powerful 'why'.

A lot of players come to The Texas Baseball Ranch looking for some help because of arm issues, in some cases very serious arm issues. Others have been snubbed because they don't throw hard enough. Both of these are very strong 'whys' for some athletes who don't want to these to be obstacles any longer on their path.

Whatever it is you are involved in, especially when something is not going the way you'd like, the question is "Why do you want to do this?" "Why is this important?" If you struggle answering that question then you should 1) spend some more time thinking about it and determine your 'why' or 2) consider doing something else.

How to we know if we have found our "Why"?

For many people, the first 'why' is not deep enough. Although it's good to have a starting place, it doesn't fit Coach Wolforth's "Have a <u>big enough</u> 'why'".

For example, I ask a young person, "Why do you practice?" A common answer is "Because I want to be a better player." The sequence would continue as follows:

> **Me:** Why do you want to be a better player?
> **Player:** So that I can become a starter.
> **Me:** Why do you want to be a starter?

Player: Because I have a better chance to be seen by colleges.

Me: Why do you want to be seen by colleges?

Player: Because I can get a scholarship.

Me: Why do you want a scholarship?

Player: Because my parents aren't going to be able to afford to pay for college and the scholarship would provide me the opportunity to get a college degree.

Now, we're getting somewhere. That's a pretty big why! So if we started with the question again, "Why do you practice?" and the bigger why is "It helps me to improve my skills to a level that I can be a starter and have an opportunity to be seen by college recruiters who ultimately can offer me a scholarship that will help pay for my college education".

Most people start with the 'how.' "How do I do this?" "How do I do that?" The question in return is, "Why do you REALLY want to do this or that?" Once you determine a big enough or strong enough why, the how becomes evident.

Let me be very clear, this is an emotionalized 'why'. Not just something that sounds nice or makes you look and feel smart by saying it. **It must be felt down deep in your gut. It must truly move you.** That's when you know you have a big enough 'why'.

So, if you are struggling to focus on something you think you really want, ask yourself why you want it and are doing it. Really ask. By keeping the why alive you might just be surprised where it takes you.

Once a player has a map, and a "big why" what other challenges might they face that they need to be prepare for?

Like many young men we work with, our son wants to be a professional baseball player, ultimately a Major League baseball player. He realizes it is going to be a challenge and has worked extremely hard and will continue to do so in pursuit of this goal. When it comes to dealing with naysayers, EVERYONE faces it at some point.

At school, he was assigned to complete a Career Project, starting with a career outline. This outline was to provide information relative to the career the students wished to pursue. It included information on prompts such as the type of degree that would need to be obtained, how long it takes to obtain that degree, what schools are best known for that degree, as well as things like why the students were interested in that career and what skills they have that suits them for that type of career.

Garrett, of course, put his as "Professional Baseball Player", completed the rest of the outline accordingly and received the following response:

"Not what I was hoping you would do for a project. Chances of this are slim. I want you to think of a career that is reachable. Don't get me wrong – shoot for the stars! In the meantime..."

Think of a career that is reachable?! I guess his teacher looked at the numbers! Between the Minor Leagues and the Major Leagues, there are approximately 5200 players. If we narrow it down to just the Major Leagues then were looking at 750 players.

Ok, so I guess maybe it's not reachable. He probably should have selected something more along the lines of a neurosurgeon since there are between 2800-3500 of those. I don't know. That may still be pushing it a little too much.

Ahhhh, I got it. A more reachable career would be that of an astronaut. It's impressive too. Those guys have a lot of stature. Oh wait, there have never been more than 150 astronauts at any given time.

Oh my, what else could one aspire to be. What about a politician, perhaps a U.S. Senator? There are only 100 of those and that makes a governorship out of the question when you consider there are only 50. There are so many things that are simply "unreachable."

I guess some people just can't help themselves. This person obviously thinks this advice is helpful. Thank goodness she wasn't around when Christopher Columbus was setting out to cross the ocean, or when our Founding

Fathers suggested we gain independence from Great Britain, or when we decided to send astronauts to the moon.

Is she right? Are the chances "slim"? Certainly, but we could provide a whole lot of examples of chances being slim that succeeded. It is moments such as these that we should be thankful. First, when more people think like this, we get a definite advantage; they are beat before they ever get started. And second, they give us fuel for our fire.

Do you have any tools that can help young athletes overcome the naysayers?

Just ask the question *"Who made THAT rule?"* Take a look at the following picture of young soccer player, Gabriel Munoz. Do you see anything missing?

The answer obviously is his feet. He only has stubs. If you hadn't seen the picture and I asked you if someone without feet could run or actually play soccer, most people would say "No". Well, he does and at a competitive level in Brazil. If you know anything about Brazilian soccer, you know it's pretty good.

So, while most people would say, "No, you can't play soccer without feet" our response should be "Who Made THAT Rule?"

I've got many other examples but here's another one of my favorites. I think most people would say someone would have to be out of their mind to think they could shoot a bow and arrow without any arms. Even if they managed somehow to do it, they could not possible be good enough to compete in the Olympics. "Who made THAT rule?" Certainly not Matt Stutzman.

He not only competed in the Olympics, he won a silver medal. To me, these are very inspiring stories. I don't know about you but they give me a quick reality check when I start to have any doubts about something I'm doing or finding difficult to do. So, just ask yourself, "Who made that rule?"

What about athletes that have the fire and are working hard, but they still feel like they are not making as much progress as they want?

There's a saying that, "He who is good with the hammer, thinks everything is a nail." What that means is, we often can get caught in tunnel vision. For example if you are going to a hitting instructor, they will mostly be looking at your it's just mechanics." But you could have great mechanics, and poor eyesight that is preventing you from seeing the ball! That's where most pitching instructors are operating as well, "I'm just going to teach things that are all mechanics."

Our bodies, including our brains, are much more sensitive than that. **Your success in sports is only *partly* based on your mechanics** or your mastery of skill.

---

9 Foundations of Successful Athletes

1. Warm Up Rituals
2. Body Care and Recovery
3. Mobility and Flexibility
4. Strength and Stability
5. Conditioning
6. Personal Body Structure and Alignment
7. Winning Mindset
8. Nutrition, Hydration and Sleep
9. Personal and Spiritual Integrity

Part of getting an effective workout, being an effective athlete or becoming an effective leaders is understanding and seeing the big picture of how all elements of these elements work together. Try looking at your challenges from a more holistic standpoint and you may find something that you didn't originally see on the surface.

Do you have any advice for athletes that have already experienced some success but want to keep growing?

I recently got to hear the celebrity country music singer/songwriter John Rich of the duo Big & Rich. His story is one of rags to riches. He grew up in a trailer park in Amarillo, TX and now has a home in Nashville with a pool on the roof. On the surface you might think, "Wow, how lucky is he!"

Yet, once you listen to all he did on "his way up" there's no doubt he deserves every bit of his success and it certainly wasn't about luck. For example, he wrote over 500 songs before he had one become a hit. That's right, more than 500. There are a lot of aspiring songwriters who have written 50, 75, 100 songs with no success. They then throw up their hands saying, "It's just not meant to be" or "I'm not getting any breaks" or "I've worked so hard and people just don't appreciate my talent." We can always come up with excuses. John Rich did not.

He shared many things about his business and career but the most interesting comments to me were his thoughts on what you do once "the ball starts rolling". You know, when you get over the hump and things start to go your way. When you're seeing and reaping some success.

For a lot of us, we give a big sigh of relief. We're pleased. We take note of what's going on and work at staying on course. Other people (and what I often see with many athletes) have the attitude "I've arrived. I no longer have to work as hard. I don't need to prove myself." As the late great motivational speaker Zig Zigler said, "that is "Stink'n Think'n".

John Rich took the concept and catapulted it. He said, "Don't watch the ball roll, KICK IT! After you've kicked it, strap on a rocket and light it." In other words, supercharge it. Use the momentum and go to overdrive. When hearing this I thought "of course". Yet, I realized, I personally can do better in this area.

He also made another point related to this that I believe is critically important. He said, "Once the ball is rolling and YOU can't keep up to kick it, GET OTHERS to kick it with you." Again, I believe this is very important and a lesson I've had to learn. As you grow and expand, you're going to have to ask for help to continue that growth. This is why you need a League of your own!

Let me be absolutely clear though. First, you've got to do all that you can do. Remember, it's your ball that's rolling, own it!

What are your final words of wisdom for young athletes that want to live a life of impact?

One of my personal mantras is "Where there's a will, there's a way." I remind myself of it constantly when things aren't quite going well. Sometimes it takes a little extra sweat to break through. Sometimes it takes a little more thought. Sometimes it takes the help of others and sometimes it takes stepping back, temporarily removing yourself from the situation, saying a little prayer and coming back refreshed.

I also love this old fable...

One day a farmer's donkey fell into a well.

The farmer frantically thought what to do. With no solution, the farmer regretfully concluded he should give up the idea of rescue, and simply fill in the well. Hopefully the poor animal would not suffer too much, he tried to persuade himself.

The farmer and his neighbors began to shovel earth into the well.

When the donkey realized what was happening he wailed and struggled, but then, to everyone's relief, the noise stopped.

The farmer looked down and was astonished by what he saw.

The donkey was still alive and progressing upward. The donkey discovered that by shaking off the dirt instead of letting it cover him, he could step on top of the earth. Soon the donkey was able to step up over the edge of the well and he happily trotted off.

Life tends to shovel dirt on top of each of us from time to time. The trick is to shake it off and take a step up. I encourage you to determine how you can shake any dirt that's being shoveled on you. Remember, where there's a will, there's a way.

Sample Ah-ha's with Coach Jenn:

1. You have to have a map! It's okay to start drawing a map with what we know. We must work to improve our map by measuring our progress with tools along with guidance from experts and coaches.

2. When faced with voices of doubt ask:
"Who made that rule?"

3. When struggling to make a break through, look beyond the mechanics, you may just be a millimeter off.

4. Once we start having success, keep kicking the ball!

We may have a vision for ourselves, but once we get the ball rolling Coach Jill said get others to kick the ball with us. We must surround ourselves with others who hold themselves to high standards of excellence and share a positive vision for the future. **That is the definition of a power team.**

In the next chapter, we'll discuss the most challenging parts of working with a power team, and how you can become a leader!

Meet Coach Karen

One of the most challenging parts of working with any team is bringing individual expectations and personal goals to form **one single cohesive vision**. This is what great leaders do every day. I'm excited to introduce you to a very special personal mentor of mine, Coach Seimears. As a high school student, Seimears gave me many unique opportunities, she challenged me to go beyond my comfort zone and she lead by example.

If you remember in last chapter, coach Jill asked the power question: *"who made that rule?"*

Coach Seimears is a MASTER at this question. As a successful filmmaker, a collegiate tennis player, a teacher, a minister, 4x World Champion Quarterback in women professional football, mom and career woman.... she has never let anyone else set the rules for her life. She lives the #LOYOlife.

In this chapter Karen shares:
- ✓ How to lead a team, even if you are not the best athlete on the team
- ✓ How champions use warm up time to get an edge
- ✓ Insights on how to get along with a coach you don't understand.

5. LEAD LIKE A QB

A Conversation with Coach Karen Seimears...

I was always throwing a ball against the house or anything I could find. I played basketball, softball, and volleyball. I chose tennis over track, because I didn't want to run that much! I ended up going to college to play tennis.

After I graduated things changed. There was a huge void in my life. I missed the competition and the teammates. The friendships I made with my teammates were irreplaceable. One day I was in the checkout line at a grocery store and saw the cover of Sports Illustrated with news of a women's football league starting.

I drove about four hours for my first tryout in Houston, Texas. I played for Dallas for eight seasons and then coached there for two. When I think back on the greatest moments of my entire life, my sports memories are at the top of the list

What does it take to build a championship team? What makes a championship team different from the rest?

Most people don't know professional women's football exists! When you play professional football, you play because you LOVE IT! It takes a special leader to bring women from different backgrounds and professions, mold them into a team and compete at a high level and win championships.

If you were an athletic female, could run and jump, and weren't afraid of getting dirty, we could find a place for you on the Dallas Diamonds. But to be the best, it took more.

When we began meeting teams in pro bowls and All-Star games, they would ask what makes us different. Family was always at the top. I would have done anything for the person to my left and my right. Many people say that, but not many people MEAN it and ACT upon it in their daily lives.

What does leadership mean to you, and how can young athletes step into a leadership role?

When I started playing with the Dallas Diamonds, I was not the best athlete on the team. I wasn't even the best quarterback. I won the starting position four games into the season. My teammates would tell you it was leadership over talent. That's hard for me to admit because of my ego. I would like to think I was the best ever to play the game. Realistically I wasn't!

I will say this. I have more trophies than anyone. We have more championships than anyone and I have more MVP honors than anyone else on my team. It was all because of leadership.

We had a girl on our team who was so fast I could toss her the ball and she would run by everybody. The problem was she would just drop the football somewhere along the way. That's really, really bad. I would go up to her before every game, take her hands and tell her she had the best hands in the league. She was not going to fumble. Some of my teammates would roll their eyes and give me weird looks when I did this. I had two choices; I could either help her believe she was going to hold onto that ball or I could roll my eyes and give her attitude. If I rolled my eyes I would have taken away a possibility for one of our teammates with the potential to be one of the best athletes in the league.

There was another girl who was just a teeny, tiny skinny girl. She wanted to play tight end. She had the height for it, but wasn't strong. More importantly, she wasn't tough. In football, there are times you just have to stand there to protect the back when you know you're going to be hit She sometimes wouldn't give up her body and do what she needed to do.

One game I grabbed her face mask and pulled her as close to my facemask as I could. I used the meanest voice I had ever used. I told her that if she would play like I thought she could play she would end up being one of the best! Five years later she tried out for Team USA who plays football globally and now has a gold medal.

She called me and said, "Hey I'm an alternate for Team USA." I said, "Sorry," because I knew that wasn't her goal. She replied, "No, I went from really stinking to being an alternate for the best football team in the world!"

Being willing to encourage people is a big deal. You can decide whether you want to jump on the bandwagon and give someone a hard time for something they're not doing well, or you can choose to be the voice in their ear when they're in that really critical situation. They can know you are the person who really believes in them. If somebody believes in you, you're going to try harder because you don't want to let them down.

To be a leader you have to be willing to our work everyone else all the time! I hate to say "you needed to go the extra mile" because it's a cliché, but it is true. I think every athletic poster and T-shirt says it. Being the best took a team of people willing to put in more hours than anyone else. It required people willing to watch more film than anyone else and to work out in the weight room longer than everyone else. Are you the first one to practice? Do you have your stuff together? Are you the last one to leave?

I was putting in the work even though I wasn't the best athlete. I worked harder than everyone else on the team, except the weight room, which wasn't my favorite. There I worked out AS hard as everyone else. I watched more film. I studied more. I was willing to accept critiques on my game, which was the hardest part for me. My end goal was to be the best. In my desire to become the best I was willing to put my pride aside, listen and make it happen.

As a leader, what are some specific things you would do to mentally prepare before a game when you showed up early?

For football there's a lot of studying to know the plays. If anybody got there early, especially the younger players, I would sit with them and talk about plays.

I would do a lot of reflecting. I think people are starting to understand the mental game is critical for success. I would sit down with teammates and talk about specific situations in the game. What did they see? What did they think we should have done there? What were ways we could play better?

Sometimes we would beat somebody 50 to 3 and they would tease me about how I didn't ever lighten up. Not every team is going to be easy to beat. We won many games, but those victories were easy because we consistently put in the work.

I would run, because I was not the fastest person. Sometimes I would spend extra time stretching. If I knew my back was hurting, I would make sure I was stretching my back even while visiting with other players. I never wanted anyone to think, "Wow she was just goofing off at the beginning of practice and now she's hurt all of the sudden." Perception was important. I always wanted people to know I was trying to lead by example.

How do you bring in new people to your team and give them a vision of what you think your team is capable of?

Do not be afraid to have private conversations with people. I tried to spend time with everybody. Sometimes that's hard because you don't like everybody. Let's just be honest! We all have different personalities, and most people don't have the personality to get along PERFECTLY with every single person they meet.

To bring new people into the team you sit down, look them in the eye and talk about your goals. You have a conversation about who you are as a team and what you want as a team. For us as Dallas Diamonds, those conversations sounded like this: "We are champions. We are the best. We work harder than anyone else." I would also always follow that conversation up with, "If you need help, if you are having a hard time. I am a resource for you."

It's about respect. I may not agree with you, and I may not like what you're doing, but I understand and respect that you bring something of value to my team. I understand I need you and that if we don't do this together we're not going to be any better. That shared vision cuts through much of the fluff. As long as you're here to win and I'm here to win, I can deal with some of your quirkiness. Every rookie either knew it and understood it, or they knew it and left.

What was your relationship like with your coaches on the team?

I respected all of my coaches. As good athletes we sometimes have more of an ego than we want to admit. We have to keep it in check. I had this one coach I swore was just trying to break me down! I thought that he was trying to take away everything that I did well and make me something that I wasn't

About three-fourths of the way into the season we were playing a really tough game. He came up to me and said, "All those things I've been asking you to do all season don't think about them right now. Just go play." I ended up having a great game. He called the plays I wanted. He gave me the ability to do the things I really wanted.

After the game, I had a little bit of an attitude, but I would have never said anything. I was thinking, "SEE! When you let me do the things I'm really good at, we do really well." But my coach pointed out something that changed my perspective. There were a few plays that didn't end in a touchdown but he showed how we made gains when, in the past we would have done poorly.

He said, "If I just keep letting you do the things you're good at people can predict how we play. If we work on things you're not as good when playing lesser opponents, then when we get to the tough games you can use these other skills."

I wish he would have told me about that at the beginning. It goes back to that shared vision. They want to win and I want to win. I have to assume that I don't see the bigger picture. I'm just a player and they are managing all the players. It was a really big learning opportunity for me.

When I became a coach I tried to be up front with players. I could understand how, as players we sabotage ourselves. If my coach HAD told me "Hey, we're going to work on all of your weaknesses," I don't know if I would have been as willing to give it my all as I was by being left in the dark about it.

How DO you communicate with your teammates or players? How do you handle it when you have to deliver a tough conversation?

I am a communicator. That's just one of the things I am. As a coach, the hardest communication problem I had was when one of my players had a concussion before a big game. The doctor evaluated her, but she couldn't pass this concussion test.

Instead of the doctor telling her, I had to. I NOW realize when coaches have bad news to tell us, it hurts coaches more to tell it than it does as players to hear it.

As an adult player, I didn't cry a lot. As a coach, I would have to choke it back all the time. Telling someone she can't play is tough when you know they've worked so.

I wish I would have given my coaches the benefit of the doubt more and understood they hurt when they told me things I didn't want to hear.

BONUS QUESTIONS FROM GIRLS LIKE YOU!!!!!
Kyleigh V: As a girl in a boy dominated sport what encouraged you to keep playing?

I didn't feel like I was breaking any gender rules or setting any standards. I felt like I was trying to get a first down. When I was a kid in my neighborhood all the little girls and boys got together and we played. They didn't care if I was girl. They just thought, "Man she can fling the ball down the field."

Sometimes people would ask, "Are you guys as good as the boys?" I would say, "That's not the point. We're not trying to be as good as boys. We're trying to be the best girl's football team in the world, period".

Lexi M: As such a busy person, with a big vision, how did you manage your time? Do you have any time management tips?

That was the hardest part. I don't want to tell you guys that I studied my playbook when I was at work because I don't want you to study your plays when you're at school. Let's just say sometimes I was creative.

When there are priorities, you make them a priority. When your mom and dad are running your schedule you have to have open communication with your parents. You say, "I know these things have to happen, but there are things I have to do." I would go to my mom and say, "Mom I have all of these things to do. How am I going to do it?" She is great at helping me get clear on what is important and make good decisions.

Morgan M: How do you keep from getting frustrated when you know you're not playing your absolute best?

I guess I would ask, "Why do I not want to get frustrated when I'm not playing to my full potential?" There's no one in this world that is harder on me than me. The trick is how to handle that frustration.

We had a playoff game where I stunk. It was the only time in my whole career I've ever been booed on the field. I remember it like it was yesterday. I didn't want to go in the locker room because I was embarrassed to see my teammates. Instead of being frustrated and pouting and sulking, I worked out. I worked on the things I had messed up. I got better. What you learn is how to harness that frustration and change it into something positive. I don't think you shouldn't get frustrated when you play poorly. I think that you should be frustrated! But the question is, "Are you going to let that frustration cripple you to where you can't get better?" Will you take frustration and channel it into creating a positive outcome?"

Aryonna B: How important is leadership to you in your life now?

Well today, I work for Apple in an administrative role. I help schools figure out that technology is great in class. I have to be a leader. I think a lot of people see leadership as walking in front of everybody and blowing the whistle, or carrying a flag. Leadership is about sitting back and listening to what everyone is saying then adding your opinion where it actually helps. **A good leader listens more than she talks.** Listening is the most critical skill to being successful. You have to be able to listen to the wisdom of those around you.

Write your "Ah-Ha's" or Questions Here:

_____

_____

_____

Ready to Play Up?

YOU could be featured in our next book.

Find out more in the #LOYOlife Action Guide

Log in with your parents at
www.LoyoBook.com/guide

70

All-Star
RELATIONSHIPS
/ˈrəˈlāSH(ə)nˌSHip/ noun

1. the way in which two or more concepts, objects, or people are connected, or the state of being connected.

-the way in which two or more people or organizations regard and behave toward each other.

-an emotional and association between two people.

Synonyms: connection, relation, association, link, correlation, correspondence, parallel, alliance, bond, interrelation, interconnection

What does it mean to have
All-Star Relationships to you?

Submitted by

JENNA SHERRARD, 9

" Friends no matter the score, or the team"

❂ RELATIONSHIPS

In this section you are going to learn how to build amazing relationships and build a power team so you can see your vision come true.

In life, we find ourselves on many different teams. From school projects, to sports to, working with your family, the way you develop relationships will greatly impact the quality of your life.

Think about relationships like the **seats on a bus**. (The #LOYOBus!) You can drive, you can ride shotgun, or you can take a back seat. Regardless of what seat you choose to ride in, *your seat gives you a unique perspective.* A good seat provides proper support and is comforting.

Like good seats, good relationships keep you pointed in the direction you should be focusing. They have a seatbelt that is not to snug for the day-to-day drive, but they will hang on to you tightly when your life is on the line.

In this section you'll learn how to put yourself in the driver's seat of life. **The first person on your team is you.** If you want an amazing team, you must be a great teammate first. *This is where we will start*

Meet Jenn Holt

Have you ever been in a situation where you felt like you weren't acting or performing like yourself? Maybe you have felt distracted, stressed or pressured to perform at a high level, while balancing the many responsibilities you have on your plate. If we don't learn how to handle this pressure, it can have devastating effects in our relationships!

Healthy relationships bring out the best in us; they leverage our strengths and develop our weaknesses. Just like all things in leadership, there are things we can control and there are things we cannot. In any relationship, the only thing we can control is *how we show up*!

Jenn Holt shows up like no one else! A former Division I softball catcher, Jenn is a MASTER in sports psychology and biomechanics. (Which basically means she knows more about both how your brain works and how your body works than 99.99% of the people in the world).

In this chapter, Jenn shows you:
- ✓ How to unleash your inner warrior
- ✓ How to balance many responsibilities with less stress
- ✓ Three easy-to-remember steps to perform better under pressure

6. WHAT'S IN YOUR BAG?

A Conversation with Jenn Holt...

I was coaching college softball in southern California and our players were smearing eyeblack on their faces and then applying loose glitter on top of it in many crazy colors. Our locker room was a mess. Glitter was EVERYWHERE. Finally, I pulled one of the girls aside and asked what she was doing and if she understood the purpose of eyeblack? She looked at me and smiled and said, "Coach, it's not eyeblack... it's Warpaint."

At that moment a huge light bulb went off and I was pleasantly reminded why I adore female athletes. You blaze trails, you work with what you've got and you make it happen. Although I appreciated the loose glitter, it mischievously traveled my skin for weeks even though I wasn't wearing any! It was clear to see these softball players had a strong sense of pride in their team, school colors and themselves. When I played softball at Cal State Fullerton, I would have told you that I bled blue and orange and if I had the opportunity to wear my team colors I did so at every chance.

As I watched these softball players mix eyeblack and glitter together, it dawned on me that these athletes were simply trying to convey how they felt on the inside by showing it on the outside. These young women were Warriors. They were Warriors on the field and in life and their creative, expressive glitter proved it. I searched high and low for eyeblack in different colors and was surprised when nothing existed. It felt like such an obvious idea that should exist for all athletes, competitors and fans alike to express their inside Warrior on the outside.

So, I did what any sane softball coach would do, I set out to create a product inspired by the Warriors I had around me. In 2013, I began my entrepreneurial journey and launched *We Are Warpaint*, which defines eyeblack in color. This journey has been one of the most rewarding adventures, because I've had the opportunity to observe individuals choose certain colors and personalize how they make their mark, by making We Are Warpaint a part of their 'Warrior identity'. How cool is that?

The pride of We Are Warpaint is how simple it can be for individuals to shift from one identity to another. It's interesting to see how something as simple as eyeblack and glitter can transform even the most shy athlete, into a focused and confident Warrior on the field.

What do you mean that you have seen athletes shift from one identity to another?

Usually, when we talk about relationships we focus on the relationships we have with other people. But before you can understand the relationships you have with others, you need to understand the relationship we have between you and the things you care about.

When we peel away all of the layers that make you extraordinary, there is A LOT inside of you. You are very complex! You have so many identities that complete you as a person and each of those identities have unique responsibilities. Every responsibility you have requires a different type of effort and attitude.

When you are not clear on your current identity or role, it leads to frustration and even failure. For example, have you ever been in a softball game, about to go up to bat when you find yourself thinking about something that happened at your last at bat, or an error made when you were on defense? Did that help you or hurt you when you went up to bat? Or at school, have you ever been in a math class when instead of paying attention to the lesson you are trying to study for the test you have in the next class.

These examples might not seem like they have much to do with our relationships, but they do! The habits of being a great student, or a great hitter, are the same habits it takes to become a great daughter or friend. Have you ever had a conversation with a friend, when all of the sudden she pulls out her phone to respond to a text and she stops listening to you? How did that make you feel? If you made your friends feel this way all of the time, do you think they would want to spend time with you more or less?

Defining the identity you need at the time you need it is essential to putting you in the best position for success. If you want less stress, better relationships and more success in everything you do, we must master the art of shifting identities to the task at hand.

The question to ask yourself is, *"What identity do I need to be in the moment it's needed?"* When you're able to clearly define and shift into the identity that matches the present responsibility, you'll be able to reach your goals faster!

When I was a freshman catcher at Cal State Fullerton I tore my meniscus in my right knee and needed surgery. At that moment, my core identity of being a softball player hadn't changed, but my definition of that identity shifted to injured athlete in recovery.

The goal was simple. I wanted to get strong and healthy so I could return to the ball field. With my identity clearly defined as an "injured athlete in recovery," I was able to create a game plan. It helped me to stay focused on the things I could control. Because I was clear on the responsibilities of my identity, I was able to recover as efficiently as possible and get back to competing at the game I loved.

What happens if we don't learn to understand our identities?

Imagine if you had a giant, heavy book for every identity you have. Picture squeezing all of these big books into one enormous bag and then slinging that big, heavy bag over your shoulder to carry with you everywhere you go. Imagine if you had to run the basis with that extra weight on your back. Imagine trying to study, play with friends and take a test with this big heavy bag on your shoulders. It would make you tired and sore! Yet that is how many young high performing athletes are. We feel like we have to carry around the weight of the world on our back 24/7. You are probably carrying around extra weight at times you don't need to. This weight is called worry. Worry leads to fear and is the biggest killer of dreams.

When we try to deal with our identities out of context they start causing even the simplest tasks to become difficult. Eventually you will experience exhaustion, overwhelm or burn out. You will be unable to perform at the levels you want in any area of your life.

So what can student-athletes with many identities do to make life easier now?

Simply because you are reading this book, I already know you are an extraordinarily strong person. You choose to carry a bigger, heavier bag than the average person. You may juggle more responsibility on a daily basis, than some of your friends juggle in a week. Without a plan, this can make it difficult to keep roles and identities separate from one another when you need to focus on a specific task. That is why it's imperative to invest time developing the following 3 habits so you're able to complete your responsibilities to the best of your ability. All you have to remember is to check your B.AG. Brand. Activate and Grind.

Step 1 is to Brand

Brand means to name or mark in a way that cannot be forgotten. List all of your identities and give them a name so each role is clearly defined. Be specific about what your *brand* means to you and the characteristics you want to embody.

For example, your *Brand* list might include:

> **Softball Player:** Coachable, Vocal, Aggressive,
>
> **Daughter:** Patient, Good Helper, Appreciative
>
> **Student:** Alert, Inquisitive, Helpful
>
> **Friend:** Energetic, Caring, Good listener

This activity can help you play better too! I played softball for 15 years and continually battled separating my performance on the infield from my performance in the batter's box. It became a vicious cycle of either living in the past or worrying about the future. Either way, both scenarios I was not where I needed to be. I needed to be present.

The sweetest thing about sport and life is we usually have more than one opportunity to make the necessary shifts in our identities so that we can embrace the challenge in front of us. When I found myself living in the past or future, I would ask myself what *Brand* of softball player do I need to be in this present moment? Do I need to be a defensive softball player or an offensive softball player? I could even get more specific. I could ask questions like, "In this situation, do I need to be a patient hitter or an aggressive hitter?" Answering that question allowed me to work the next step of the identity process, which is the *Activte*.

Step 2 Activate

Activate means to excite. So when we activate an identity, we are becoming excited about what we need to focus on so we can perform at our best. Once you recognize which BRAND identity you need at the time, you can activate by using a trigger to help shift into that identity. Think of it like a superhero that activates their superpowers.

For me, balancing a full academic load along with the responsibilities of being a Division I catcher put a lot of responsibility on my plate, especially because our softball season was at the end of the school year and regionals were always during school finals. Regardless of the academic responsibilities I had, when I walked into our Titan locker room and put on my softball jersey I was no longer Jenn, the student-athlete, I was Jenn, the Division I catcher for Cal State Fullerton.

When I transitioned from my school clothes into my Titan uniform, that was my trigger to activate the identity shift I needed to help me shed the weight of my bag as a student-athlete, friend, daughter, etc. and focus on one specific identity. The same held true after softball games when it was time for me to be a student. Once I removed my Titan uniform, cleaned up and put on my school clothes, I was ready to put my softball identity back into my bag and retrieve my student identity.

Step 3 Grind: Lastly, it's not enough to simply *Brand* your identities and activate them once. If you want to live the league of your own lifestyle you also have to *GRIND* at your identities. *Grind* means to sharpen.

You can sharpen your identity by becoming clearer about your responsibilities and characteristics. By layering on multiple activations that help get you focused and by reinforcing those activations.

Just because I say I'm a present-softball player, doesn't make it so. I had to *work* at focusing and re-focusing on being the best collegiate catcher I could be. If we don't grind at and continually sharpen our identities, our heavy bag of responsibilities can still become a distraction. So, if I use my Titan uniform as a trigger to activate my desired identity, then I can grind that activation by tucking in my softball jersey to remind myself that in this moment I am a Division I catcher for Cal State Fullerton and I am present.

As you get older and take on new responsibilities your bag will get heavier. There is a possibility that the weight of new responsibility could you distract you from your vision. What separates the good from great is how quickly you can Brand, Activate and Grind the appropriate identity at the time it's needed. If you consciously practice these 3 steps with each identity in your bag you'll find that you're able to enjoy a more quality relationship with less effort. These habits will give you more quality time to focus on the things that matter to you most in sports and life.

What are your final words of wisdom for any athlete that is ready to re-define who they are and lighten their bag?

Be where you need to be, when you need to be there. Be a softball player when it's time to be a softball player. Be a friend when it's time to be a friend. Be a daughter when it's time to be a daughter and so on. Don't rob yourself of having a quality relationship with someone or something you love because you haven't taken the time to dive into the details of what each identity means to you.

If one of your identities in your bag is being a daughter then ask yourself what kind of daughter you want to be and then work hard to make that identity a reality. It's easy to want to be a loving, appreciative daughter, but it takes a plan and working the plan to BE a league of your own daughter. When you start setting aside appropriate time and focus for each role in your life you'll find that you'll start to enjoy each relationship more and feel more refreshed about investing in other relationships and identities in your life that help you become the best version of you.

Write your "Ah-Ha's" or Questions Here:

_____

_____

Ready to Play Up?

In the LOYOlife Action Guide you'll find out how you can work directly with amazing mentors like Jenn every month!

Log in with your parents at
www.LoyoBook.com/guide

Meet Jami Lobpries

Now that you have a clear idea of who you need to be and when you need to be there, the next part of building relationships is making sure that who you are and the inside is the same message you are expressing on the outside.

Jami Lobpries is a branding expert for the national professional Fastpitch League. In the past, she has been responsible for sharing what makes each athlete in the league unique and expressing up with the rest of the world. She has done great growing opportunities for you in your future and now she's going to show you how you can use the same strategies to do the same for yourself by leveraging your own personal brand.

In this chapter, Jami will show you:
- ✓ How to leverage social media for scholarship money
- ✓ The #1 thing that communicates your brand everyday that you may not be aware of
- ✓ How to support your team when they are down.

7. A LONG TERM BRAND

A Conversation with Jami Lobpries...

I'm from a small town near Houston, Texas. I grew up playing every single sport you can imagine. I'm probably the most competitive person you'll ever meet in every area of my life. I've always been a good student. I wanted to be number one in my class. While I was healing from an ACL injury, I channeled my competitiveness into school. This resulted in becoming more interested in academics.

After getting healthy I had to choose between collegiate soccer or collegiate softball. I chose softball. I went to Texas A&M in 2004. I went with a class of four. You may have heard of Amanda Scarborough and Megan Gibson; who in my opinion are two of the greatest softball players to ever play.

My freshmen year, I was the only freshman who didn't start and didn't play. It was a difficult role for me. I found myself sitting the bench. I had to redefine my role and who I was going to be. It made me work harder.

As a team we experienced many successes. In 2007 we went to the Women's College World Series. We went two and out, but it was fun. In 2008, my senior year, we had a strong vision and goal of playing for a national championship. We lost the national championship, but it was still a really cool experience. I put my cleats on home plate because I thought I was done with the sport of softball.

As I headed to grad school, I got a call from the National Pro Fastpitch league to continue my career. I didn't want to lose out on that opportunity. I played four years in the NPF. I experienced success on the field, but more so, I had the opportunity to see what was happening in professional softball. It was such a cool opportunity. I knew women athletes deserved the opportunity to call themselves professional athletes.

I have dedicated my life to growing women's professional athletics. I went back to Texas A&M, where I recently obtained my Ph.D. I taught sport management at the University of Tampa where I did some branding and marketing for two professional softball teams, *USSSA Pride* and the *The Dallas Charge*.

Mentally, how did you handle going from being a star on one team, to being a role player in college without letting it get you down?

It was a very humbling experience. In all facets of life you have a choice. I could have pouted and been a bad teammate. I chose to redefine who I was going to be on the team. This was about creating my brand, defining who I wanted to be, and how I wanted to be perceived by my teammates. Today I believe not starting was one of the best things that ever happened to me. I had to be humbled.

What is personal branding and why is it important to young athletes?

Your personal brand is your identity. It's who you are. When somebody says "Jami Lobpries," what does another person think? What image am I portraying through my actions? That's what I call your brand, your identity or your image.

As girls we learn not to talk about ourselves and not to speak "about me." We're taught to speak about "we", collectively. You need to think about what you as an individual are portraying to others. What are you portraying to your teachers? What are you portraying to your parents? What about that college coach who is trying to recruit you? What image are you establishing?

Your brand is everything you are putting on social media, what you're saying, what you're wearing, and who you're hanging out with. It's also your non-verbal actions on the field. These say so much about your character, about who you are. No matter where you go in your life, even if you aren't going to play college softball, your branding is important. How you express yourself to others impacts what college you go to, what jobs you get, how teachers interact with you and what friends you attract.

College coaches are looking at social media profiles when they are recruiting. How could the things young athletes post on Instagram or other sites impact their future?

You have an online history. When I was a college coach, we looked at what potential recruits were posting. You have this timeline college coaches look at to see what you were posting a year ago. We learned a great deal about the players we were considering recruiting through social media posts.

Look at your timelines and other social media and ask, "What is my timeline saying about me?" Take your last six pictures on Instagram. What is that saying about you? Do you have pictures with your family? Are you playing sports?
If you have pictures you wouldn't be proud to show your parents or future coach then change what and how you post. Your profile is very easy to find.

How can we use social media and our image as a tool to help us stand out and allow other people to see our growth?

You have an opportunity through social media to show your character, to show who you're proud of being. Take pictures of yourself taking extra reps of practice, working out, and studying for school. Those things send a positive message. What story do you want to tell about your life? Put a little humor in there. Ask yourself what it is YOU want to portray to the world.

Do you have any real life examples of how social media has impacted players you know?

I coached at Division 1 University and was in charge of monitoring Facebook. I had an 18-year-old freshman post a picture of her drinking alcohol.

I told her, "What if we're playing an opponent, they print that picture, and blow it up. How embarrassed would you be to have this picture of you doing something illegal showing on the field?"

On the flip side, I coached 12-year-olds last year. They had some of the coolest posts. They talked about passion. They posted pictures with teammates and added really cool quotes to it. These 12- -year-olds were posting such inspirational messages. I like the positive route of what you can do with social media.

How does our image impact the type of people who decide to be on our power team? How does it impact the type of friends we have?

Being a girl can be tough as an athlete. You want to fit in. Part of your brand is staying true to your *core values*. Your brand really is the core of who you are. Think of what's most important to you in the long term. If your ultimate goal is to get a college scholarship, then you have to remain true to who you are on social media.

You have to post things that represent what you and your family are proud about. Those things are so important and can get lost in the day-to-day.

I want to hang out with people who make me better. I want people who are going to push me and inspire me. It goes back to one of my core values of being competitive. I want to be the best. I don't have time to hang out with people who are going to make me a worse version of myself.

What other specific things do we need to be aware of which impacts our future? How can we create the best opportunities for ourselves?

My college coach, Jo Evans, was the best role model I've ever had. She said there are two things you can control; your attitude and your effort. I think that goes with every single thing you do. It's attitude and effort in school; attitude and effort on the field, off the field, with your friendships, your teammates... everywhere.

One of the most important things is your non-verbal communication or body language. Your body language says a lot about who you are. Are you tired? Not listening? Do you walk with confidence? It's something we aren't always aware of.

When I was about 12, I would get pulled out of a soccer game because my body language portrayed me being a bad teammate. Inside my head I was thinking, "No, I'm competitive. I want to be on the field." My coach pulled me aside and made me aware of what I looked like to others. It was up to me to make that change and make that adjustment.

You can have accountability partner, someone who is watching, to help you become more aware. Being aware of poor body language and being willing to accept feedback can be tough. Being open to criticism that can help you reach your goals really helps.

What's something we can do as teammates to help make sure our team image is what we wanted to portray?

If your team has a goal, ask what you are doing collectively to reach that goal? If you have a teammate who's getting out of line, and isn't on board working towards that goal, then you have a responsibility to approach her. There are different ways to do this. You can have a conversation and say, "Are we doing our best to reach our team goal?" It's tough to say things that might feel uncomfortable. But again, you want to *think long term*. You grow when you are able to step out and make one of your teammates better, just by speaking up and communicating. As long as you communicate in the right way you are going to make them better. When your team wins, you win too.

As a teammate, what does that communication look like? Let's pretend we are sitting on the bench in a softball game, and our coach decided to pull our pitcher. She comes into the dugout and sits down and puts her face in her hands. What could we do in this situation to be a good teammate?

First, know your teammate. Some teammates might need a couple of minutes to cool off. If you know that, then wait a minute or two. Approach your teammates when they are by themselves. Don't call them out in front of the team. I would go over to my pitcher and say, "Let's think about the big picture. You're going to get your moment to go back in. You're going to help our team win. Maybe it's not right now, but your moment is going to come and you're going to help us win."

As I mentioned, when I was a freshman, I didn't start. In the post season, our center fielder got hurt and I went in to play in a regional. I was struggling one game, so my coach pinch-hit for me. The girl who pinch-hit for me hit a game winning home run. Instead of feeling sorry for myself, I was so proud of her because we won the game. I'll never forget that senior coming up to me after the game and saying, "Next year is your year. Help lead this team." She empowered me by reminding me I would help lead the team in the long run.

Ready to Play Up?

In the LOYOlife Action Guide you'll find more information about how to stand out from the competition.

Log in with your parents at www.LoyoBook.com/guide

BONUS

AH-HA MOMENTS WITH GIRLS LIKE YOU

Every month, girls just like you have live-private group video chats with our Legacy League mentors! On these calls, you get to ask questions and get help with any challenges you are facing! **Here are some of the major Ah-Ha Moments girls like you took away from their group time with Jami Lobpries!**

Lexi M: age 14 *Indiana*	I took away that I need to be careful with the things that I share on social media. I should be aware of what I post or what I say verbally especially when I am emotional because it tells a story about who I am..
Katie S.: age 12 *North Carolina*	What I learned was just in case you're not in the spotlight that that doesn't mean you're not going to be or you can't help ...I can talk to my teammates and keep them focused on the long term.
Rinn M. Age 9 *Oklahoma*	I took away that everyone is different and there are different ways to handle people when they're down.

Knowing great information and DOING it are two very different things! In the next chapter you will see *what can happen in your life,* when you apply the lessons in this book! Lexi joined The MVP Leadership Academy - Impact program just a few months ago and she has a really powerful message to share with you today!

8. THE TEAM YOU CAN COUNT ON

A #LOYOlife story By Alexis McClure, 14

I believe you should fight for the things that are most important to you. For me, family is one of those things. Six months ago, my life was a mess. I was trying to balance multiple sports teams, keeping up good grades and find time to fit in extra curricular activities. I was beginning to feel overwhelmed. It was almost like I couldn't catch my breath. I couldn't even remember the last time my whole family had dinner at the table together to talk about our day. We had all become "too busy" with our day-to-day responsibilities. It took me a while to realize how these extra commitments began to change my personality and impact my relationships with the people I cared about most.

I remember the first time I felt the desire to really make my parents proud. I put my softball bag in the back of the car, got in the back seat and I looked my dad in the eyes to tell him I wanted to play with a different team. I was only 10, but I knew I wanted to be part of a team that had a passion for the game and the desire to win. My dad challenged me and asked, "Lex, are you sure you want to take this big step? Are you actually willing to work hard and fight for your position?"

I thought about his questions carefully before responding, " I know it is not going to be easy but this is something I really want. Dad, you are my inspiration! I want to show what I can truly do. I am willing to work hard and fight for my position."

There were hundreds of people at my first tryouts. I was nervous and scared. I had never seen so many girls all playing the same game at one time. I knew for me to succeed, I was going to have to fight through my fears. I did my best while the coaches evaluated my form, my effort, and my skill. As the tryouts began to wrap up, I did not have a good feeling about my chances of making the team. For the final drill, I waited patiently in long line, while the coaches began to hit hard ground balls to each girl before me.

All of a sudden, it was my turn. I was down and ready... Before I knew it, I had a fat lip! The ball had hit a rock and bounced up to hit me in the face. I had bit through my tongue! I did not cry. I could not feel the pain at all. The whole right side of my face was numb. *(Unfortunately, I was not wearing a mask either. Wearing a mask was just not something we thought about in my previous league. Sometimes in order to take your game to the next level, you need new tools for protection!)*

After I took the hit, I asked the coaches if they would hit me a new one. I was bleeding from my mouth and spit blood out onto the dirt. The coaches were hesitant to hit me another grounder. But, I got back in place, got ready and asked them again. They hit me a new ball, I completed the play perfectly and got back in line.

The call came a few days later. I had made the team. They said they enjoyed my performance and my perseverance through the hit. They stated that the reason they took me was not because of my skills as there were many others who had far more skills than I did. They said, "Skill could be taught, but a *no-quit* attitude and is something that could not be taught."

While I am a contributor to a team I love today, making the transition to travel softball hasn't always been easy. It took me several seasons before I found a team that was right for me, but it was never something I would give up on. That first year, I sat the bench a lot. I put in many hours of extra effort to earn a position on the field. It just seemed the results I produced were never enough! Season after season, my coaches would drop me for any taller, stronger athletes that came along. I had many broken hearts and many tough lessons. I felt like I would never find a team I could count on and I found myself on the bench far more than I wanted to be there.

Have you ever felt like you have been "benched?" Not just benched in softball, but benched in life! Think of a time when you really want to go spend time with friends, but your parents said "no!" They might even have a really good reason for saying no, like making sure you get enough rest for an upcoming game. Still it can be frustrating when you feel like you are missing out. This is exactly what was happening with me just six months ago. When my parents would say no, I would get mad, and I would argue.

I really hated fighting with my family, so I started isolating myself at home. I would go up to my room and just listen to music. I wasn't really opening up to my parents about things that were going on in my life. I was scared that if I asked them a question and didn't get my way, I would just get mad and cause another argument. So instead of working on communication and understanding, I just decided to shut them out.

I know what it is like to feel shut out. I mentioned I spent many of my early days of softball riding the bench, but I learned something very valuable from that experience. My dad showed me how I could use my time on the bench, as an opportunity to listen to the conversations between coaches in the dugout. I tried it. I learned by listening I received valuable information about what it took to be successful on the field. With that information, I learned sitting on the bench in the dugout doesn't have to be the death of a softball player. I am here to tell you, that next time you are feeling "benched at home", it doesn't have to be the death of your social life either! In fact, it can be the best time for you to build those relationships that matter most!

It was about this time I joined MVP leadership academy and started working with a mentor. I felt a connection with her right away! I could open up to her about how I was feeling overwhelmed with school and softball, and she understood where I was coming from. On our first private call, I shared how I was missing family dinners and how I really wanted a stronger relationship with my mom.

My mentor shared some tools with me that helped me to find clarity around what was most important to me. Here is an easy exercise she taught me that you can try now: Imagine yourself fast-forwarding through your life. See yourself at your prom. Now going away to college, falling in love and finally moving into your first house. Imagine a day when you really need your parents, and you are looking at the phone getting ready to call them. When they pick up, what is the conversation like? How do you feel about making that call? If you were to keep acting like you do today, what would that conversation be like? When I did this exercise I realized how essential it was for me to have a strong relationship with my parents, and I definitely had to change.

Just because the ball hits a rock, doesn't mean you quit on the game you love. Sometimes, your relationships will take a bad hop too. I've even learned there's times you just have to bite your tongue, but that doesn't mean you have to put on headphones and shut out your best team mates. That can be the best time to listen and learn! Remember, skills can be taught, but never *ever* quit on the people that love you the most, they are the team you can count on!

What does it mean to have All-Star Relationships to you?

"It shouldn't matter the outcome, but rather how well you and your teammates can play together."

Submitted by

AUSTYN MATLICK, 17

All-Star
EMOTIONS

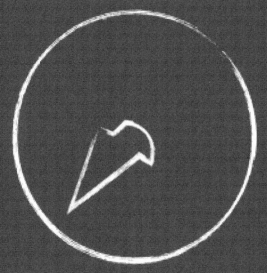

1.   a natural instinctive state of mind deriving from one's circumstances, mood, or relationships with others.

– a conscious mental reaction subjectively experienced as strong feeling usually directed toward a specific object and typically accompanied by physiological and behavioral changes in the body

synonyms: feeling, sentiment; reaction, response. passion, strength of feeling, warmth of feeling, instinct, intuition, gut feeling; sentiment, the heart

What does it mean to have
All-Star Emotions to you?

Submitted by
CAYLEE GILLIS, 12

✪ EMOTIONS

Nothing has more power to impact how quickly you can reach your goals that the way we understand and influence our emotions. Emotions directly impact our thoughts, or beliefs and our actions.

Think of your understanding of emotions like understanding how to turn on the windshield wipers on your vehicle. Not understanding your emotions can make it feel like you are driving in the rain without windshield wipers! You definitely want a tool to help you see when its pouring and you are trying to get somewhere safety!
Things happen in our lives, especially in our relationships that can drastically change our beliefs around what we are capable of.

In this section, you'll learn ways you can actually change the way you feel about your current situation, your future or even about the past. If you've ever woken up on the wrong side of the bed, and had a horrible day as a result, this one is for you.

Meet Coach Stacie

In this chapter we'll build on what we learned about relationships and how our relationships can impact our emotions and confidence level. I'm excited to introduce you to the lady that just "gets" you, Stacie Mahoe.

While she grew up playing softball on the isolated islands of Hawaii, today she is hyper connected with people from all around the world! Stacie helps parents and coaches by providing them with resources so they can better support you as an athlete! (She has a lot of practice with connecting sport families because she has eight children of her own!) Talk about #LOYOlife! If you have ever felt similar to the way Lexi expressed in her personal story or have a desire to have more energy each day, Stacie can help you!

In this chapter Stacie shares:

- ✓ A simple strategy to boost your mood on rough days so you can feel happy more often.
- ✓ A pre-practice ritual that will help you get more out of practice and play better in high stakes game situations.
- ✓ One simple way to open up a difficult conversation with family, even if you have never shared your emotions with them before.

9. THE "AWESOME SAUCE" HABIT

A Conversation with Stacie Mahoe

People said, "Do something you love." I love to read and I love softball. So, I started jotting down some lessons I learned along the way. I wrote things I thought would help other people and I launched my website. I share from my experiences and encourage coaches and parents to raise champions, not just for sports, but for life.

Today, sports have become so competitive, especially with the Internet and our hyper connected world. Obviously, there's good that comes from this, but it can also make things more challenging for you as a player. For example, when a college coach sees a great athlete from a certain school, they don't have exclusivity. If there's a great player out there, everyone knows about her because she is on YouTube! This has made getting to that next level even more competitive.

So there's so much more pressure for you as a younger athlete to stand out, no matter what the sport, to catch the attention of college coaches much faster, much earlier. I think it's very, very easy to get caught up in all of that as a parent, and as a player, and lose perspective about what is most important.

Your parents want what is best for you, and they work hard to help you achieve your dreams. But they're being told from so many different people all kinds of things they 'need' to do in order to be a great parent! Kind of like being in the batter's box and having five coaches all yelling different things at you. It's just a lot of pressure all the way around.

As a young athlete, what do we need to know about how this new environment is impacting the way we grow up, make friends and develop into leaders?

Today there are so many ways you can compare yourself to others! Before, you could be the best on your team or the best in your league and you could feel great about yourself! But now you can see what's going on in other cities, states and countries! It's easy to say 'well, there are so many other people out there, kids out there, who are doing what I do'. It's easy to get caught in the trap of comparing yourself to others, which contributes to the fact that most athletes drop out of sports by around age 14. You have lots of time to develop and grow, but you have to stay focused on _your_ game!

It's important to remember, when people post on social media, they don't post everything! When was the last time you posted a video of yourself striking out? Probably, never! When you look at social media, you're only seeing highlights of everyone else game! You don't see the errors, the mistakes, or the bad plays.

When you only see the "ESPN Plays" it's easy to think 'well I don't stack up to that, how am I ever going to be good enough'? But that's just not a fair comparison. After all, you make great plays too!

The other thing you may not realize is your parents feel the pressure too! For a long time, I would think "am I doing good as a parent if my child isn't achieving x, y or z. Only recently have I realized that what my child accomplishes or doesn't accomplish has nothing to do with how good of a mom I am. Once I was able to separate my child's achievements from my worth and value as a mom, I began enjoying my time with my kids more and helping them enjoy their journey too because we could just focus on the games we love!

And that is what helps you become as great as you can be in what you do! You've got to love it! It's got to be something you really want, something you pour your heart and soul into. When you let too much of that outside pressure creep in, you lose that. Playing for those outside pressures and expectations instead of for your love of what you do is not going to give you that result that you're after.

What other things should young people know about social media, outside of sports?

It's super important to remember social media is just a glimpse into other people's lives, that it's not their whole reality. If you're feeling down or stuck, or like your instagram photos aren't as fabulous as one of your teammates, just remember that no one posts their strikeouts! If you choose to focus on the places in life where you feel you are struggling, your life may feel a lot worse than it really needs to.

What other areas of your life have you noticed that only having one perspective has caused you frustration or pain where it wasn't necessary?

I've been married to my husband for over 18 years. We were married young, so there have been a lot of ups and downs and learning and growth in the relationship in general. Relationships evolve over time.

There were so many times my husband would say something and it made me feel bad. When I finally built up the courage to go to my husband and say 'hey, you know when we were talking about this...it made me feel bad'. The reality was, the way I felt was far from what he intended. If I had never brought it up to him and voiced my feelings out loud, I would've never understood his side of it, which was not even negative! He was actually coming from a place of love, that's just not what I felt or how I received it.

What I've learned is our perception of different situations or of someone else's words, is received only from our own personal viewpoint. Think of it like looking at a ball being pitched over home plate. Is the pitch an inside pitch, or an outside pitch? It depends on which side of the plate you stand on! It's the same pitch but it could look differently to me than it does to you! If you can just suspend your feelings for one second and consider that there may be a whole other side to the story, if you can open up your mind to accept that 'okay, what if it was meant from another way? You can save yourself a lot of grief. If it's ever possible, find out what was meant from the other side, or talk with people you trust, that can help you see a different perspective you may not see on your own.

For me, that's been critical. It's important to have people in your life who have been through similar experiences and can share a totally unique perspective. That is one of the reasons it's so important to have a mentor and to be plugged into an empowering community. Their input may help you see hope or opportunity that you didn't see before.

How can we relate this back to playing sports?

When you play sports, you must consider every situation from a team perspective. Your coach might have a chance, right now, to get somebody else some playing time and strengthen your team in the long run. Just because you get taken out, doesn't necessarily mean that you did badly, did anything wrong, or that the coach doesn't trust you. There are other things going on at the team level, remember to keep that in mind instead of taking everything personally.

We all go through ups and downs emotionally, what is one thing that you think could help a young person shift their emotions, when they feel they are really struggling with negative emotions like stress, anxiety or even depression?

I wish someone had taught me this earlier! You're constantly getting evaluated, especially as a student-athlete. Your schoolteachers give you grades; your coaches give you playing time. Well, one thing that I've started doing recently, to help shift my own perspectives, is to write in my "Awesome Sauce" journal.

So every single day, I sit down and I just write down the good things that are going on in my life, or in a particular area. So, I'll write down things that went well, little victories, big victories. Anything that made me smile, feel happy, these are all things I can build on. These are all things that I want to do more of. I also include things that make me feel better, more relaxed and less stressed. It could be as simple as "I had time to get out of bed slowly today, and that feels much more relaxing than jumping up at the sound of the alarm and rushing off to brush my teeth and rushing to get ready for the day." Become aware of those little things that add stress to your day, versus opportunities to feel more relaxed. By jotting those things down, you build a better relationship with yourself. You get to know who you truly are better.

What we focus on expands. Where our focus goes, energy flows. When you write down all these awesome things, you help yourself cause more of those things to happen in your day. You can construct your days differently. You can handle your relationships differently. You can make different choices and create more enjoyable days or more enjoyable experiences more often.

What kind of changes have you seen happen in your life since you started writing in a journal?

Last year, I wrote down some pretty big exciting goals for myself. Since writing in my journal, I'm able to see the progress towards those goals so much clearer. When you do this, you begin to see things happen more effortlessly. Things just seem so much easier. It's not that I don't have struggles. It's not that I'm not having obstacles thrown in my way. It's not that life is suddenly perfect, but I'm able to see the path toward my goal totally lying out in front of me so much clearer. It gives me confidence because I can see myself actually getting there. Making the commitment to journal helps you focus your thoughts and your energies and that makes a big difference.

What are other things you do to shift your emotions?

If you look at the word e-motion, it's really just energy in motion. If your energy is "blah", your emotions will be "blah" too. You're not just going to flip a switch and have the emotions you want magically appear.

One day I was at a conference and before every speaker came up they had everybody stand up and clap and whoop and holler as loud as possible. It created a lot of energy in the room. So one day we I decided to incorporate this into our team practices. Think about the energy at your team practices. You just got off of school and you may be tired. This is not the same energy you usually have before a game, which means it would be impossible for you to practice how you play. Try it for yourself with your team before your next practice.

Get really loud and celebrate as if you just won the season championship. Just something as simple as starting off with a cheer changes the feeling and the energy and the vibe of the whole session. We start practice like that every single day and it makes a really big difference.

That's why athletes like Tiger Woods always do a fist pump; it's an action that is invigorating. It energizes them and they begin associating that movement with something powerful, with something upbeat, with confidence. So they can use that physical movement to feel better.

It's not always easy to shift your mood, but you can actually have an impact on how you feel and that's what's great about it. But it takes practice. It's okay if you're 10, 11, 12, 15, 17 and you're not perfect at it yet. I'm almost 40 and I'm not perfect at it yet. It's still something I must consciously be aware of and do on purpose. So if you're not perfect at it, it's okay, just keep practicing.

What are some of the things that can happen to us if we don't learn to manage our emotions, especially in this highly competitive environment?

Your repeated emotions have a direct impact on your beliefs about yourself. If you are always beating yourself up, you aren't going to believe you are worth much. It can very easily just become a downward spiral. You might start believing other people can achieve things but somehow you can't. These negative voices can easily get out of control and take over.

Your health, your actual physical health, can be damaged. You're not going to be as healthy when you're stressed out. Think about it. If you don't think you are worth much, you often don't even bother with things as simple as getting a good night of sleep, drinking enough water, or making good food choices that fuel your body. All of those simple everyday tasks become more difficult when you don't feel good about yourself.

So when you're not aware of the effects of your own emotions, it becomes like quicksand, and it can be hard to pull yourself out of it. If you feel like dropping out activities you used to love, or if getting up in the morning to brush your teeth and get dressed to go to school becomes a monumental task, you know you are in trouble. It's time to start changing something in your life.

When you start going down that path, it opens you up to the negative influence of people that may not have your best interest at heart. You might start spending time with people that don't really care about your goals. They probably have struggles in their life too and they're just trying to get by. They want you to join them because it makes them feel better but it's probably not really what's best for you.

For me as a parent, it's super important that my kids feel I'm someone that they can talk to even at their weakest, or lowest point. They can tell me anything! I am part of my kids power team! It's important for YOU to build that power team around you.

A power team includes people you feel like you can be yourself around and be vulnerable around as well. It's important for you to DESIGN that power team NOW. You deserve to be surrounded and supported by people who love you on your good days and on your bad days. You don't have to wait until your bad days to start building your power team.

Sometimes as young girls there are things we feel like we can't really tell our parents. We are scared they might be disappointed in us, or even angry. What if we have

something we really WANT to be able to open up about, but we don't feel like we can?

That feeling is totally normal. And, maybe you do have a reason to feel scared. Maybe you have had a past experience where you've tried to share something and it wasn't received well. Remember back to our conversation about perspective!

I wish I could say 'you can always go to your parents and tell them anything. They're going to love you anyway' but I don't know that for sure. Most likely, if you are reading this book, you have a very supportive and loving family. But sometimes families have their own challenges and struggles. That is very common too.

There are so many parents who really love their children, but don't always have the tools to respond in the way that they should or they could. They don't always respond well the first time they encounter a new parenting challenge. As parents we are learning too!

If you have something you know you parents aren't going to be very happy about, or when they say something that upsets you, keep in mind that the reason they respond the way the do, is because they love you so much. To you it might seem over the top, but children can scare parents! Sometimes fear takes over and we (parents) respond in ways that are not ideal.

You may not fully understand that now. Just know, most of the time, when your parents go over the top, it's because they love you so much and really don't want anything bad to ever happen to you. Anytime they feel that life may be harder for you as a result of a poor decision or mistake, they feel like they failed you somehow. Maybe they weren't able to help you get through high school more easily, or get you through social situations better, or get to college like they hoped they would. When you feel like you have failed someone you love more than just about anyone in the world, it hurts. That pain or frustration a parent feels can look like anger toward you or disappointment in you.

As parents we get upset when we aren't able to do everything we hoped we could do for you. We feel like we let you down. To you, that might feel like mom or dad being mad at you. If you could look past all that, you would see love, a lot of love. We (parents) just don't always communicate that effectively. We make mistakes too.

There have been times when my teenagers have come to me and said "You know Mom, when this happened and we went through this situation, you didn't even come in and help me out, I feel like you didn't have my back!" I was like "Whoa, okay. Well, that's not even what I meant by that. I didn't come in and rescue you because I fully believed you could handle that situation on your own. From my mom perspective, I had full faith in you and felt that you didn't need my help." It was just a total miscommunication and two totally different perspectives on both sides. That's how far off perspectives and perceptions can be, even in relationships as close as parent and child.

Most likely, your parent is open to hearing your perspective. They may not even realize what message came across to you. If you aren't sure on how to get started talking to them, ask them if they would first mind reading part of a chapter in this book that has been really helpful to you. Ask them if after they read it, if it would be okay to have a discussion about some of the things you learned! This can be a great icebreaker to open up about some of your feelings.

Have you ever been upset with one of your kids for coming and sharing from an honest, genuine, kind place about how they have been feeling?

No, it's always been eye-opening for me. I totally appreciate my kids expressing how they feel in a situation. I've thanked them numerous times for them giving me another perspective and a second chance to better explain what I meant. That helps us build a better understanding of each other. I can apologize and I think that's important. I apologize for the way I made them feel. We all learn and grow from that.

What are you most grateful for in your life today?

Without a doubt, it's always my family. They bring happiness and joy and smiles to my day every single day. It's not always the big stuff, but the tiny little moments. As hard as it can be to have a big family, and as stressful and hectic as things can get, I wouldn't have it any other way. We are each unique.

I believe each person has their own gifts and their own strengths. I believe that about my children. I believe that about everyone's children. I believe that about everyone in the world. You have a unique gift inside of you and the rest of us need it from you. We all need you to let your gifts and talents out, to be who you are, so we can enjoy the amazing value that you have within.

Write your "Ah-Ha's" or questions here:

_____

_____

 Ready to Play Up?
In the LOYOlife Action Guide you'll find 7 Confidence Hacks!

Log in with your parents at www.LoyoBook.com/guide

Meet Coach Nicki

If you still are not sure if you can control your emotions, let me introduce you to somebody that will help you begin to realize just how powerful you truly are.

Nicki's story started as a youth softball player just like you and while she went on to play Division I softball, she had to overcome some enormous health challenges that could have cost her life!! She is now the founder of The Next Generation of Softball in Pennsylvania, a new kind of travel program that strives to prepare young athletes to play softball at the highest level, while promoting life skills, discipline and education. Nicki chose to use sports as a tool to make her feel better, she has definitely lived the #LOYOlife!

The next time you're just not feeling up to practicing, or not feeling like you have the energy inside you to give it your all, Nicki's story will help remind you what you're truly capable of.

10. DO WHAT YOU CAN DO

A Conversation Nicki Starry...

Softball was always a way of life. I know a lot of young girls feel the same way. At nine years old, I was diagnosed with leukemia. I was playing softball at that time in San Diego, with my sister. Bridget was a pitcher and I was a catcher. When you are sick, sometimes you do not know what is going to happen the next day. The doctors said, "You do what you can." So my family encouraged me to continue to play. I just didn't know my little body could do so much.

The softball field was one of those places where nobody was sticking me with needles, nobody was telling me I was going to die. I could just be. The rules of the game never changed. It was always 21 outs. I was always really grateful for that time to where you could just shut off outside world. Then, in turn, I got to do some really cool things.

The doctors gave me about 60% chance to live, at least until I was 15. They caught it late. They weren't too hopeful, but they said they had some new experimental treatments we could try. We chose to be part of the trial. If you have ever heard of anyone say "CHEMO". Chemo really does kill everything in you. That's why many people loose their hair. I lost my hair twice playing softball, and while treatment really was horrible, I'm alive and very grateful for it!

I would go to the hospital in the morning for treatment. The doctors said if I could keep myself from throwing up, they would let me go home and I could go play. I would grit my teeth and pretend as long as I could so I could get out of there.

When you are in physical or emotional pain, it can sometimes be challenging to keep a positive mindset. How did playing sports help you feel better?

One of my biggest memories was one of the first times I remember actually sitting on the sideline because I was just so sick. I had gone in for a heavy-duty treatment that morning. Our team was losing. Of course my teammates would never ask me for anything, but I could feel their motivation going, I could feel the game going. I asked my mom if I could play. She said, "You can do whatever you can."

I remember just getting to be back in that dugout with them. That was bigger than anything for them. It had such an impact on how they felt. It was bigger than that for me, because I didn't feel sick anymore. I was there with them. As a team, that was it. We won that game.

Just by going in the dugout, you didn't feel the sickness in your body that you felt when you were sitting on the sidelines?

It was gone. Just being able to be near my team and feel that camaraderie makes you feel better. Then the adrenalin of the game starts pumping, and you can see it in everyone's eyes. The rest of the world just goes away. That's one of the reasons it's so important to have a team around you. When you go through tough times, it makes things easier. It makes the pain not so bad.

At the time it didn't make sense to me when people would want to write articles, and people always wanted to hear my story. In my brain, I was a kid who just wanted to go play softball and to be healthy. It didn't make sense to me not to play. It made sense to go be like everybody else. That was it. I was going to fight as hard as I could until I got it. It's important to remember that we all have our own challenges and adversity, just stay focused on going after what you want most! Do the things that make you feel good, and invest time with people that make you feel alive.

Do you think staying in sports helped you become a healthy teenager?

Sports taught me how to fight. True athletes are able to turn on that switch in your brain where you push beyond what you think you are capable of. Like when you're training and your body wants to stop, but you've got to keep going. You get in those moments to where it's a tie ball game and you've got to ignore everything else around you. That is what I did in my brain. I focused on little things I had to do to overcome slight obstacles so I could reach my goal of later that day. I think as athletes, we all have that power with in us!

What would you say to those athletes that are dealing with a big challenge in their life and they feel like they are on an emotional roller coaster... How can they stay focused so they can get through it?

First, keep your focus simple when it comes to the things you need to focus on. Often we focus on the things we don't need to focus on. Then you start to feel in "overwhelm." When you feel overwhelmed, it doesn't make sense when someone say, "Life is hard, and anything hard is worth having."

When it's right in front of you, it just seems like the biggest obstacle you could possible overcome. That's why I have the girls I work with journal, because for the most part they don't talk until it's too late. As I say talk, talk, talk often, and talk early. Communicate about anything. Start with small things.

What are some everyday challenges that you think we need to have more conversation about?

Self-image is a BIG ONE. How do you see yourself? Recently I went back and read through my old journals. Some of the biggest events in my life, I only talk about in two or three sentences. The boyfriends, the breakups, best friends, the drama of the day, that's what took up pages in my journal. I look at the girls I coach now and that's what affecting them in their everyday life too.

I think kids now and young adults even into their 20's struggle with "how do other people see me? Am I going to fit in? That's tough. That's tough for anyone.

We have to remember that we all are amazing people. We can really learn to respect each other first. Humanity does really win out from there. In Next Generation of Softball, we've created a community where the girls get to really know each other without judgment and begin to understand each other. That's not easy to do.

From a leadership point, I love what you are doing with All-Star Club, because you're giving each girl a chance to learn how to lead and share with each other what they're feeling. I think that's going to take them so far and that's what's really going to make these women and young ladies just soar.

You have a very powerful story, have you found that when you share something to personal that people interact with you differently?

They do. When I was younger, I shared my story more often. It was in the papers. Then I became very self-conscious of it because it seemed everyone then had these expectations of me. I was having trouble living up to being me. When I received a scholarship to play at the University of Wisconsin, I didn't let them share my story. Anything at Wisconsin had nothing to do with my cancer. I just didn't let them talk about it. I really needed my time there to find me! Not who Nicki Starry the cancer patient was, but who Nicki Starry was, as an athlete being in college. I'm really grateful for that time.

I'm even more grateful for people like you who now help me to share my story. Now that I am in my 30's, I love where I am at today and want to remind every young athlete that even us strong ones now struggled with who we were. I extremely struggled with weight issues, with self-esteem issues, with public speaking, with all these things that you may struggle with. We're human, too, but if we can do it. You can too!

What would you tell a young athlete that feels overwhelmed with everyone's expectation of who they are supposed to be or become?

I see this every day! When an athlete comes up and shares this emotion with me, the first thing I do is give them a BIG HUG! I know how hard of a conversation that can be. Here's the truth. You can't live up to anyone else's expectations. Set yours first. Where do you want to be? It's going to change. I promise you all. It's going to change, because life changes, you change, life grows and people grow.

I think this big picture of who we think we are supposed to be and become overwhelms us. Start right now to do the things you're looking forward to. What do you love doing? What makes you passionate? What do you love in school? I really do try to have the girls I coach break it down to the simple stuff. If you like something, try an internships Try things early on in your life, this will really help you find clarity when the time comes to make these bigger decisions. Then hopefully there's not so much pressure. The softball part should be the fun part. The sport part should be the fun part.

If you could leave every parent and every girl you meet with only one piece of advice what would it be?

This game is a HUGE game of failure, so practice letting things go. If any family's anything like mine, you take it home way too much, way too often. I tell my parents today how much I appreciate how far they helped me get. My advice to my parents when I was younger would have been to give me a little bit more grace. There is no one harder on me than me for a little while.

If you commit, the lessons from this game will set you up for the rest of life. Please coach it forward, pay it

130

forward, because those coaching right now are doing the best they can to help you make an impact, to push you forward, and they're probably not getting much in return. If you do anything for the game, for yourself, for those who are giving it to you now, coach it forward, play it forward. It's all I can say.

Write your "Ah-Ha's" or Questions Here:

_____

_____

_____

Ready to Play Up?

Find out how you can take control over your your own emotions and feel better more often!

Log in with your parents at
www.LoyoBook.com/guide

In the next section, you will read a special story from a girl just like you! I first met Mara when she was just 11 years old. **If you ever come to one of our live training events, you might hear me tell her very funny "Woo-Hoo" story**. Mara was one of the VERY ORIGINAL ALL-STAR club members; back before all-star club was a "thing". She let me experiment on her with crazy brain hacks when I was first learning about mental toughness and building power teams. I'm honored to introduce you to an original all-star!

11. FOR THE LOVE OF IT

A #LOYO life story By Mara Miller, 16

I wasn't really into sports all that much as a little girl. In fact, the only reason I became interested in softball was from watching my brother play baseball. From there, I decided that I wanted to try softball, even though I was a little older than most of the girls and they had already been playing for a few years. It turned out that I was a natural, and softball became my favorite pastime. I started taking lessons and playing select ball, spending all of my free time just having fun with the girls I was playing with. Then, around the age of 12, it seemed like instead of just playing to have fun, the game evolved into a means to an end; and people played solely with the intent of getting a college scholarship.

The emphasis placed on sending emails to college coaches and forming relationships with them seemed to be the most important part of playing the game, and that kind of ruined the fun of it for me. The part of me that loved to play the game got lost in the sea of correspondence with college coaches, and I didn't enjoy playing the game anymore. So, after a while of being invested in that lifestyle, I decided to take a step back from that and focus on going to school for my academics and if I could play softball at that school, it would be an added bonus. This change in mindset helped me go back to just having fun, goofing around, and loving the game. Luckily, I recently found the place where I can focus on my schooling and play softball in the University of Montevallo where I am currently verbally committed.

The turning point that forced me to reevaluate my goals and intents with playing softball was during the summer between my freshman and sophomore year. The coaching of the team I was on had changed hands that spring, but I was still loyal to my teammates and I didn't want to face the inconvenience of finding a new team, so I stayed for the summer season.

That summer was completely awful. The new coaches pushed us harder than ever to send out blanket college emails to anywhere we would even consider going, and we would all get in loads of trouble if we weren't sending those out. They also played favorites worse than I had ever experienced before. My teammates began to form different cliques and turned against each other. Usually, there were at least four or five girls crying at the end of each game, no matter if we won or lost, simply because we were so beat down and made to feel inadequate. The team traveled all over the country together, and since we spent so much time with each other and the coaches, we were spiraling further and further down the wrong path. The entire team was relieved when the season finally came to an end. That was the first time that I had ever really experienced the cutthroat competition for college looks, combined with coaching that was not encouraging, and I absolutely hated it.

Softball lost all of the fun and mystery that it use to have. In a sport where failing 70% of the time is supposed to be considered good, I was miserable anytime I did something wrong because I knew that my coaches weren't very forgiving and didn't give second chances.

Spending almost the entire summer away from home put a real strain on my family relationships. My mom hated being away from my dad and brother for so long, as she was the one to come with me on all of the trips. She and I argued all the time, because she was unwilling to pay for me to play on a team where I didn't have fun or play that much, and she didn't want to put up with me crying and moping around all the time. I became estranged from my dad and brothers, because we almost never saw each other, let alone spent time together. The entire thing was just a complete mess. When my attitude toward softball started to affect other aspects of my life, such as my relationship with my mom, that was when I knew it was time for a change.

I finished the summer with that team, but then I moved on. I knew it would not be unacceptable to them that I didn't want to go play Division 1 softball. While I love the competition of the game between teams, I hated what the competition for a starting position turned me into. I decided that I didn't want to feel that way again.

I took some time off, playing as a pick up player here and there. One weekend I picked up with a team that really didn't care who I was, or what my intentions were; all they wanted me to do was play the game, and play it well. The coaches were encouraging and trustworthy, and generally just wanted to have a good time. This new environment brought me back to life! I started improving from the level I had stagnated at before, practicing with a vigor that I didn't know I still had, just because I wanted to get better, not to show off my skills to college coaches.

My stress level went from overload to carefree, and my relationships with my family improved because of it. When I look back on my experience with that first team, I regret my decision to stay as long as I did, but in hindsight it was a good learning experience because it showed me what was really important. Getting a softball scholarship means nothing unless you can be happy and have fun while you're doing it, and the contrast between my two teams helped me to see that!

From that experience, I learned that in order to succeed, I needed to surround myself with people that encouraged and believed in me. With support from others, especially authority figures that I could look up to, I could finally begin to believe in myself again. Just a small glimmer of self-confidence was enough to change my entire outlook on life. I started becoming more active in school, joining class office and student council, and my relationships with those around me changed for the better. The reserved, quiet Mara was replaced by boisterous, happy Mara, who is someone that people enjoy being around.

Another thing that my coach helped me to conclude was that my goals should be realistic. She taught me to set smaller goals that were easily reached, actually reached the really big goals. Starting off too big was part of the reason I felt so discouraged before I met my new coach. She believed in me unconditionally, whether I was coming off of a streak or a slump.

Surrounding yourself with people that love you and trust you is one of the best things you can do as an impressionable young player. Once enough self-confidence is built up, it becomes easier to deal with situations where you may not be able to choose the people you are around, like with high school ball. If even a small part of you still has that initial love for the game, then it is something worth pushing through.

Nowadays, people place too much focus on getting the college scholarship, and lose sight of what brought them to the game in the first place. When playing softball feels more like an obligation than a game, that's when you know it's time to step back and remember what it was like the first time you stepped on the field. That feeling, full of hope, life, and joy, is how we should approach every game, every inning, every at bat, because you never know when your last game might be.

What does it mean to have All-Star Relationships to you?

"In life, you have to balance your emotions and you also can't be afraid to express them. Softball is something that helps me to this."

Submitted by

KAITLYN MIXON, 11

All-Star
HEALTH
/helth/ noun

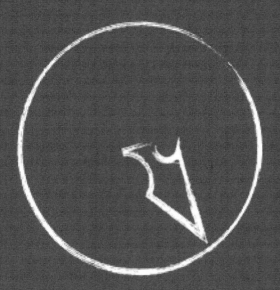

1. **The state of being free from illness or injury.**

    -   the condition of being sound in body, mind, or spirit; especially : freedom from physical disease or pain

    -   flourishing condition : well-being with reference to soundness and vigor:

What does All-Star Health
mean to you?

"Being healthy means you are fit and work hard even

after the season is over. It also means keeping my team

healthy by being a team leader who cares about your

team and try to keep them up when they are down. When

we fail, it teaches us what we need to work on. "
Submitted by
Madison Shell, 12

✪ HEALTH

When most people think of health they think of what you see on the outside; what size pants do you wear, how much you weigh or how many sick days you took this year. All of those things are a reflection of what is going on inside your body and your mind, underneath the skin. Health has just a much as much to do with your emotions, your confidence and self-talk, as it does with your diet, your workouts and personal hygiene.

Being healthy is like keeping your #LoyoBus in peak condition. You want to keep the gas tank full, the air filters cleaned and every once in a while you have to change out the oil. If you let any of these things go your vehicle will run down quicker or will stop completely.

We could write an entire book just on health for an athlete. In *A League of Your Own*, we focus on how your health impacts your athletic future. Keep in mind health can also impact your energy, relationships, emotions and your vision for yourself! If you're wondering what it takes to have a long healthy career in sports and live a long healthy life, this section will share things most people don't think to talk about.

Meet Coach Karlene

Some people believe that sports are just for children, but making sports part of your lifestyle can help you leave along healthy and fun life.

This is exactly what Karlene Headley-Cooper has been able to do. She has designed her life around her passion for sports, after playing over 10 years as part of the Great Britain national softball team. Today she is still an active athlete, teaches others how to stay healthy, strong and athletic today at the university level.

In this chapter, Karlene shares:

- ✓ The 5 main movements every athlete must master
- ✓ 3 Tips for running faster and being more athletic
- ✓ The number one question you must ask yourself to prevent burn out

144

12. POP A SQUAT

A Conversation Karlene Headley-Cooper

In Canada, they have different eligibility rules than the NCAA, so I was able to play six years of Fastpitch for the University of Toronto. Even though I grew up in Canada, I was born in London, England, which meant I qualified to play for the Britain National team. In 2005, I tried out and made the British National Team. I've just actually recently retired after 10 summers, three world championships, five European championships, two World Cups in Oklahoma and some of the just other smaller tournaments and training camps with the team.

The coolest experience I got to do was play semi-professionally for a team just west of Amsterdam. Our team was called Olympia. We played the top league in the Netherlands against some of Europe's strongest players.

How realistic is it for an athlete to play softball beyond college?

There are more opportunities than people think there are. There's a very small, elite professional league here in the States that is growing, but across Europe there are multiple countries that have leagues. You can find leagues in the Netherlands, where I went, Spain and the Czech Republic. Italy has a very strong league, as well as

Austria and Germany. I'm sure I'm forgetting some other places, but if you love softball, Europe is kind of your oyster. However so many of those opportunities are word of mouth. Having relationships with people that have been there and played is definitely important so you have a good experience. If you ever have the opportunity, definitely go play. If right now you are still working toward high school or college ball, stick with it because at the top levels, the game is growing!

What would you tell that athlete that is playing multiple sports, but is feeling the pressure to pick one and specialize?

Keep playing every sport, any sport, as much as you can. Be an athlete who's a really good softball player and a really good basketball player, and can play volleyball pretty well or really likes track; or just likes to go to the park with their family. Just be active. Those are the people that have longer healthier careers when it comes to sports. When I was in high school I played basketball, volleyball, badminton, and fastpitch. I was active in all four seasons really.

Did you say Badminton?

Badminton was actually my second sport, and I picked it up partly through my parents. My dad used to just play recreationally, along with squash. Less people probably even know squash unless you're probably from the New

England area. I couldn't be outside all year-round playing softball because eventually we have more snow and cold than there is opportunities for softball.

I would go inside and play squash. It was a great fitness thing for me as a teenager. I picked up squash when I was eleven. I had just started playing softball when I was about nine. It was something that I did recreationally in the winter when I couldn't be playing softball. That's why I'm so much of advocate for people to be active and for young girls to find every activity that they think they enjoy doing and just try and find ways to do that. Not necessarily worry so much about picking your one main sport, especially at such a young age. Do everything. That would be my advice.

How have you seen playing multiple sports impact your life now that you've played at such an elite level?

The most important thing you can do as a young athlete is stay healthy. Coaches recruit athletes. In The States, many athletes are verbally committing at a very young age. You still have got a lot of high school before you make it to college. Athletes need to keep developing and stay healthy. Continue to work on your fitness, you footwork, as well as your softball-specific skills. That will really help you make a successful transition to the college level, if that is your goal.

I've been around a few athletes who got recruited quite young. Then they sort of backed off a little bit and didn't put in the time. When they made that jump to college it was really difficult for them. They were not physically ready. So whether you get recruited young or you are still on that path to find the right fit, keep working at being as an athlete. Remember, even if you make a verbal commitment, there are no guarantees.

How important is cross training in helping to build your muscles properly?

There's more transfer between sports than people probably give credit for. To be successful you need to be agile. You need to be able to move and react. You want to be that really tough out when you get on the bases and move down the line and dive. Those things really do transfer from being a great defender on the basketball court, or being a really good digger in volleyball, or somebody who's able to run different track events. There's really great crossover in just movement that people can get from other sports. Then you just add on the sport-specific throwing and the catching and you got yourself an athlete.

You are a kinesiology professor today. Can you explain what it is and how it relates to the youth athlete?

Kinesiology is the study of movement and the idea that we want to move efficiently and effectively in ways that are going to keep us healthy and strong. What we really focus on is what we call the foundational movements. The

148

foundational movements are your ability to do five basic movements really well. You want to be able to squat, lunge, push something, pull something and lift something efficiently.

We spend a lot of time analyzing those five movements. If you think about the sports you play, just about any ready position in the field comes from a very basic athletic position, which ultimately a squat. A proper squat position puts you in a really good position to read the ball off the bat, or move with purpose in a specific direction.

We also talk about how your muscles get the oxygen that we breathe into our body, how that oxygen circulates around our body so that we can make our muscles move in the way that we want them to work. Softball is a really interesting game with the energy systems because so much of it is done in short bursts. We all know that the game lasts over an hour, and especially for some of you you're probably playing multiple games in a day and in big tournaments you've got probably more games in a day than the women's national team probably played in a week. Just being strong and healthy to last that length of time requires a different energy system than it takes to run from home to first. It's all those different components that we study in kinesiology.

What should a young athlete focus on to protect their body and be as athletic as possible?

There are three words I would focus on are pain free, symmetrical and efficient.

First, focus on moving in a way that is painless. In my kinesiology class when we are analyzing anybody's movements, if anybody experiences pain we need to stop the exercise right away. If you ever feel pain during a workout you should stop right away as well. Your body is sending a signal to you that something is wrong.

Pain is something that's difficult to understand. We may get sore and that's going to happen. We're playing a lot of softball. We're going to find that our muscles do get sore. It's important to understanding a little bit about the difference between pain and soreness.

The discomfort you feel from pain can be an ache, sharp pain at rest or when exercising. You usually notice it during exercise or within twenty-four hours of activity. You could feel it in your muscles or joints. It usually gets worse with continued activity. Soreness is different. You will typically feel soreness one to three days after your work out. This is the result of small, safe tearing of your muscle fibers. When they heal, this is what builds your muscles, along with good nutrition. During soreness, your muscles may be tender to touch and feel tight and achy. Movement may initially be uncomfortable but moving and stretching your muscles will help to decrease soreness.

The next part I would focus on is symmetry. If you always throw, hit or pitch with the same arm, you will notice one side of your body will appear stronger or more flexible than the other. When you have asymmetry in your body, or two sides that are different strengths, have different levels of mobility and stability this is when injuries are more likely to occur. Make sure you educate yourself before going into middle school or high school weight rooms, when there is often peer pressure or coaching pressure to lift more weight than your body is ready for. Get a coach in this area that is an expert to educate you on how to best build your body evenly with out hurting yourself down the road. Your focus should be on mobility and stability before strength.

Finally, when it comes to moving on the field, we want to do things as quickly as we can, but also as efficiently as we can.

Quick and efficient are connected but different. Efficiency means how much energy did you have to put in, in order to get maximum output. It's like a car with new oil will be more efficient and get better gas mileage. You want to get the most amount of mileage out of every movement you perform.

Efficiency is improved when technique is improved. For example, we were working on sprinting one day with the Great Britain Team. Our trainer told us we were pretty good, but he also said we could be faster! So what does someone need to do if they want to run faster? Most people think, well, you've got to move your legs faster. Well actually, you have to move your arms faster!

He taught us to think about putting our hands in your pocket, putting them in your pocket and taking them out of your pocket as quickly as we could That turnover in your hands will allow your feet to follow. Sometimes we think about running we think about our feet and we get caught up on our feet. We end up almost tripping over ourselves and it looks a little awkward.

Record yourself just moving on the field. Throwing, hitting, catching, base running, pitching. Whatever you do record it and watch it, that's a real eye-opening experience because you see things there that you can't see when you're doing it because you can't actually see your own body. You might notice wasted effort or steps that are causing you waste time and energy. That's why they put mirrors in weight rooms so you can see and adjust your form. Video will allow you to do that on the field.

What is the one piece of advice you want to leave for young athletes that has been big dreams and big goals to do big things?

Find some way if you can to play for yourself. I know that's sometimes hard being so young. Your parents probably often drive you places and maybe they drop you off and then go, or they stick around and they cheer for you. Whatever your arrangements might be, find something that you really, really enjoy about whatever sport you're playing.

Play it for you. Try to fill in the blank: I really like going to practice because... Think things like "I go to practice because I really like the challenge of getting better every day. I really like going to practice because I get to play softball a game I love and I get to hang out with my friends while we do it. I love softball because I can travel around to different towns, or different cities or different states, and play a game that I love." When I could say those types of things to myself, the game actually got easier. It became more fun. I had done all the hard work. I had worked hard in practice.

If you're able to fill those sentences then you've made it 90% of the way there. Taking ownership of my game at a young age could have made a world of difference to me. I love the sport but I didn't necessarily ever really think about how or why I loved the sport until later on in life.

If you can really appreciate and really love the sport for a specific reason, then I think the future of softball is in good hands. I'm excited to see the future generation of high school sports and college sports, and how the sport can hopefully get back into the Olympics and continue to grow. That's really exciting to me. If you can find that "why" at a young age, to focus on your health and love the game, literally the sky's the limit. You can dream big and there's no reason why you can't reach those big dreams. I will forever be a supporter and advocate for girls & young women playing softball.

Write your "Ah-Ha's" or Questions Here:

_____

_____

_____

Ready to Play Up?

 Download an All-Star work out you can do today, to become more athletic and efficient in the #LOYOlife Action Guide!

Log in with your parents at

www.LoyoBook.com/guide

Meet Coach Kris

You now know how important it is to move efficiently as an athlete.

If you really want your body to become the most powerful and efficient it can be we need to take a look at what is going on under the hood! The way we fuel our body has a direct impact on our flexibility, muscle health and more! Simply put, the better fuel we pick, the more efficient our body becomes!

In this chapter you'll meet Kris Massaro, the founder of Softball Strong, the leading provider of mobility training for softball players online.

In this chapter Coach Kris shares:
- ✓ 5 All Star Super Foods to help you build lean muscle so you can play and feel your best
- ✓ The truth about why flexibility isn't all it's cracked up to be.
- ✓ The #1 thing you can do to prevent injury.

13. HOW TO BE SOFTBALL STRONG

A Conversation Kris Massaro

I'm very passionate about the sport of softball. As a young girl, softball gave me amazing opportunities and brought incredible mentors in my life that opened doors for me that never would've been opened. That love has just carried on into adulthood. Now, if I can turn around and do that for somebody else, that's what keeps me going.

I love giving girls the opportunity to become better in any realm because softball gives so much back to them on the mental aspect, on developing themselves from girls into young ladies, into building confidence, and integrity, and learning to work with people on teams. So if I can do anything that helps that and helps build that and take that out onto the field, then that makes my day.

What does it mean for somebody to be softball strong?

To become a complete 5-tool softball fitness player is extremely important. It derives from components of speed, of power, mobility, mental aspect, and nutrition. We believe you can be as strong as you want to be, the only thing that can hold you back is yourself. That is why it is so important for young girls to surround themselves with a network of people that believe in themselves.

In order to become softball strong, what would you say the first area for them to focus on would be?

The biggest thing for girls to focus on is the mental aspect. As a young athlete, the more you can get understand why you are doing what they're doing, you immediately get an edge.

Let's be honest, not many people like to run, or lift weights of eat a certain way. It's not super exciting to practice your mobility. Once you understand the mental aspect of why we these things it all starts to make sense. Once you can understand how the work you put in today helps you get where you want to go, it's easier to put in more effort. Understand "the why" first, then we can really make progress!

Once we understand why focusing on our overall health is so important, what is the next focus point to master?

Our Nutrition! Sports Nutrition, the word within itself is commonly misunderstood. We should refer to the topic of Sports Nutrition as "smart eating for athletes." The food we eat is fire the feeds our body. Think of your body like a fire, got the mental image? A fire can only keep burning if you feed it; otherwise, it starts to diminish. The flames start out as bright and hot, but the flames will slowly decrease the heat that it produces will start to die down. You have to think of your body like that fire; it needs oxygen, kindling and wood to keep it burning. If your fire is your energy level, you're kindling and wood is the food you put into your body.

How do you keep your fire burning brightly?

You start by eating smart. As an athlete you are burning a lot more calories and expending a ton more energy than the average person.

As girls, you have to remember your bodies are changing and growing. Too many athletes don't get enough good food! I've seen many athletes pressured by the thought they need to be a certain weight, so they skip meals. This puts out your fire, destroys your muscle and can cause lot of other health problems. Skipping meals will actually cause you to gain weight because it puts out the fire that burns off fat.

When it comes to feeling great, feeling full and feeling energized, not all calories are created equal. Focus on foods you ENJOY that help you build muscle and stay fueled. We can call these or All-Star Super Foods.

What are some examples of super foods?

Super foods allow you to perform at your best without feeling sluggish.

Here's a good place to start;

Water, adding a squeeze of fresh lemon juice

Protein: chicken, turkey, and some select protein shakes.

Complex Carbohydrates like oatmeal, yogurt, beans & brown rice.

Lots of Green Leafy Veggies mixes with fruits like berries Healthy Fats: Avocado, Cottage Cheese and salmon.

There are a bunch of misconceptions about what athletes should eat. You may have heard the myth that you should eat a plateful of spaghetti before a big tournament. I've seen kids at the snack stand with sodas, pizza, cheesy nachos and sugar-filled candy. These are NOT ways to keep your fire burning! In fact these types of foods do quite the opposite.

They may give you an immediate sugar rush but that a big drop in energy soon follows rush. This is caused by the sugar dropping into your blood stream way too quickly.

If we want to start fueling their body for success, what is one step we can take to start making better choices?

The best way you can ensure you're eating smart is preparation. As an athlete or the parent of an athlete, start bringing your own food to games. My top choices for tournaments are: Water, Nut butter and carrots, berries, chicken breasts or deli meat & string cheese.

Remember, you can also prepare like this for a school day and notice how much better you feel in class, compared to cafeteria pizza, breaded chicken or even iceberg lettuce salads coated in dressing.

Pack mini bags with super foods in your lunch box and try to put something in your body to stoke your fire every three to four hours! You may need to plan a snack between your morning classes. Many athletes skip breakfast because they are in a hurry in the morning or they say they don't feel hungry. Then they don't eat until around noon. This is not fueling your body or your mind to live the League of your own lifestyle. Your flame is always about to go out. You probably feel sleepy after your lunchtime because your blood sugar is not balanced. If you wait until you feel hungry to plan what to eat, you are setting yourself up for failure.

Stay hydrated! Proper hydration does SO much for your body, your skin and your mind. Drinking enough water will help you realize the difference between hunger and thirst.

Remember while many popular sports drinks may taste good, they are also full of sugar that doesn't serve your body. Drinking more filtered water, you can add fresh squeezed lemon for flavor.

Most people don't realize this but hydration and mobility work hand in hand in preventing injury. The more mobility work you do, the easier you make it for all of that great hydration to work into your muscles and keep them loose and healthy.

What is there a difference between mobility and flexibility?

Yes. When we work on mobility skills, we are working more on the movement skills that we're going to take out onto the field. Mobility skills help with movement. Flexibility is more static stretching. "Oh, look. I can reach my toes and I can touch my toes," "Well okay, that's great you can touch your toes, but what can you do with that? You're still not running correctly and I've noticed that you can't jump as high. That is because you haven't been focused on working mobility for that muscle group.

So if you ever have a coach criticize you for not moving right, it might just be a lack of mobility. A lot to coaches because they put a lot of time and effort into it, because it's not their area of expertise. The good news is, there are exercises you can do to work on it!

When you are eleven or twelve your bodies are changing and as you hit major growth spurts, you have no idea what to do with all of this extra body you just woke up with! Even though you may have long lets, you might still be moving like you are shorter. So you want to do mobility excursuses that lengthen your muscles and teach you spatial awareness!

I always kind of compared it to giving a 16-year-old who just got her driver's license a Porsche. They have no idea what to do with it, and it's the same way your body.

You want to feel like if you were to hit that ball all the way to the fence and you had to run around the bases as fast as you can, you would be able to do that and not feel any pain. You should not feel tight, You don't want tight movements. You want to feel nice and loose and there is nothing preventing you from taking a long stride. Tight muscles are slow muscles; Relaxed muscles are fast muscles,

Think of your muscle groups like rubber bands. We want to stretch them out, but then they want to come right back in. If we don't keep them loose, when they come back to the middle they stay really, really tight. I would highly recommend you learn as much as you can about foam rolling and hip opening routines, You many notice that tightness your were feeling or pain you may experience can completely go away!

Why are our hips so important?

Your hips are involved in pretty much everything you're doing during softball. Most coaches tell girls "Use your legs to hit" So you don't realize that power actually starts in your hips. Your glutes or your butt are some of the strongest most important muscles in your body, most girls who have really tight hips don't even use their butt. If you were to press in on their butt, it usually doesn't feel firm at all. If your hips are tight, then you probably feel tight in your legs, and your stomachs will not be as tight as it could be because they're not engaging your core.

Our bodies are these great, well-oiled machines that are amazing, so think of a brand new car. If something breaks down in your new car a light will kick on to tell you it isn't working. That is exactly how our bodies work, but instead of a light kicking on you get a different kind of signal, tightness. If you ignore the signal, eventually your body will break down.

For example if you have knee injury, it could have started in your feet, moved up to your ankles, then moved up to your IT band. Your IT Band acts like a spring when you run, like the shocks on your car. If your hips were tight, most likely your glute med, a muscle in you butt was weak and your IT band had to do extra work to stabilize your knee. Eventually it just gives out. It's kind of like responding to the shocks on your car being too loose by tightening them up so much that they can't move. If you tighten your shocks on your car, your car has bad shocks; it can cause longer braking times and a momentary loss of steering. This is because your shocks are not strong enough to handle the weight of the vehicle. You don't want this to happen to your body!

If young athletes want to maximize their mobility and get the most out of their body, what is one simple final thing they can implement today?

Dynamic stretching! I still see team today doing static stretching before games. Static stretching is basically when you're sitting in a position and reaching. Dynamic stretching has movement involved in it. The reason it is so important is because it's preparing you for the movements that you do out on the field. I want you to be as prepared as possible mentally, but I also want to be as prepared as possible physically for what you are about to go do. The proper dynamic stretching routine allows you to get a full range of motion.

One thing that's really important in dynamic stretching, whenever you do one dynamic stretch forward, do the same thing backwards. This will help with symmetry. If you do high knees forward, do high knees backwards as well.

Most athletes tend to be front side dominant, so that means that they're extremely stronger in the front of their body versus the back of their body. This means we are creating a weakness. To be the ultimate athlete, you want your body to be balanced and equally strong, both the front and back of the body.

A good dynamic warm up usually only takes about 10 minutes. I would rather take 10 minutes and get you loose and strong than try to rush through it and not give you the opportunity to become mobile.

What happens if a girl is playing on a team where not everybody else does dynamic stretching? What would you say to her?

Ultimately you want everybody to work together as a team, but sometimes that happens. Maybe you can give them this book? Ultimately, you have to make sure that you're keeping your body healthy. Not everyone you play with will have a big enough reason why to put in the extra effort to prepare properly. I have a lot of pitchers who spend a good 20 minutes prior going through the stretches that I give them in addition to the team stretches. If the rest of the team doesn't see the value in it, I would go take some time on my own, go through my own dynamic stretching routine, and make sure that I feel good.

What would your final word of wisdom be?

I hope you understand how much you have to offer this world. We are consistently being told what we can't do instead of what we can do. Softball is an amazing platform for you to discover how much you can accomplish in school, in your careers, in pursuing your passion. If you love the sport stick with it because these tools will serve you the rest of your life.

Write your "Ah-Ha's" or Questions Here:

_____

_____

_____

READY TO PLAY UP?

 Get a copy of The All-Star Athlete Eating Plan in the #LoyoLife Guide! Plus, information on how you can qualify for a **FREE Nutritional coaching session.**

Log in with your parents at www.LoyoBook.com/guide

In the next section, you will hear from Amy, a young all-star club member who shares what could happen if you don't take care of your body!

14. FUEL FOR LIFE

A #LOYOlife story By Amy Parish, 10

 I had never pitched before. I started going to pitching lessons with Coach Jenn and started learning the right technique to pitching. I was amazed at what I could do. I started to get the idea of what pitching was for the first time. I kept going to lessons and working harder everyday. I got better and got to pitch in tournaments.

I felt like I got a reward when I pitched because I always worked hard. When I pitched, I felt my team counted on me. I challenged myself to be positive for the team. I would let them know how many outs there were, and where the next play would be. I learned this job because that was what college players do. I believe my pitching has come a long way.

One day, I got to travel to play in a world series tournament with my team. It was a super hot day and we were waiting for our games to start after several rain delays. My mom was making sure I was hydrated and eating well. We didn't eat concession stand foods or junk. Out of nowhere, I got a really bad headache. It hurt so bad, I started to cry. I never cry at softball games. So, my mom took my to the bathroom to try to cool me down, but nothing seemed to help my head. I ended up having to take a break on the bench during our final game because I felt so bad. I was not able to go into pitch.

When we got home, I learned the reason I felt bad was because even though I had been eating healthy foods, my blood sugar wasn't balanced. I learned eating just fruit isn't enough. I needed to have the right balance of food to help my have the energy to pitch. Coach Jenn helped me find a good protein drink to give the nutrients I need to play my best, all day. It tastes really good and my older brother drinks it too to prepare for his wrestling matches. I drink one before every practice and game and I always feel great! I feel like I always have lots of energy, even when my teammates seem tired and sluggish. I also drink LOTS of water. It's important for us to remember how important the food we eat is. My whole family traveled half way across the country and I couldn't play because I didn't know how to use food to fuel my body.

Last year for Christmas, my mom signed me up for the All-Star Club. What I have learned is in order to reach my goal of being a college softball player, pitching lessons is not enough. I have to fuel my body and I have to fuel my mind. All-Star Club has taught me to be a better person, never give up, work hard and stay focused on my goals. My mom always sits down and watches the team calls with me while we learn from great mentors on different topics. Make sure you fuel your body and your mind so you can be the best athlete you can be. Your team is counting on you.

What does All-Star Health
mean to you?

"Giving your body what it needs, staying active

and eating healthful foods."

MAKENA ALEXANDER, 10

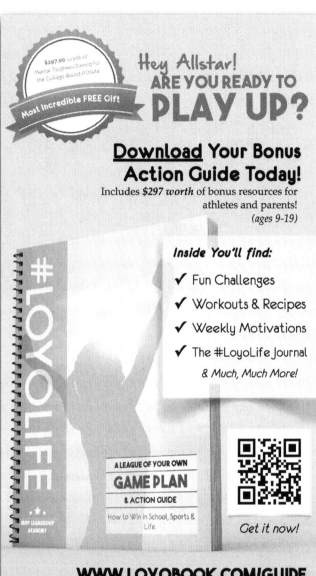
170

All-Star
CAREER
/kuh-reer / noun or verb

1. n. an occupation undertaken for a significant period of a person's life and with opportunities for progress.

1. v. move swiftly and in an uncontrolled way in a specified direction..

2. working in or committed fashion

synonyms:, existence, life, course, passage, path, calling,

What does it mean for you to have an All-Star Career ??

"An Allstar Career to me means doing what you love and only that. Life is too short to be doing something you don't enjoy. An Allstar Career is also working hard and getting what needs to be done, done."

Submitted by
ELLIE MYRON, 12

✪ CAREER

Your career represents the wheels on your vehicle that allow you to get where you want to go. In fact, the word career actually came from a Latin word the means *wheeled vehicle!*

Your career is more than just your job; it is everything that you do to make an impact on the world. This includes time invested in your education, a job, business or cause that you commit to. We also include the way to learn to manage your money so you can become financially independent as part of your career because we believe **the more money you make, the more people you can help!**

In this section, you learn from two amazing athletes, on two very different career paths. They will share how they were able to leverage their passion for sports into careers they love, that also allow them to have a positive impact on the world and how you can too!

Meet Coach Dani

If you're not sure exactly what you want to do for the rest of your life, I'm here to tell you that is A - OK. In fact, your interests and your skills will continue to change and develop overtime. Dani is a perfect example of how shifting course is not always a bad thing.

Dani is a perfect example of how you can be a role model for people your own age. Dani was this for me before she never even knew it! I had left school, about the same time Dani decided to play for the Dallas Diamonds. Because of the inspirational messages she shared on social media and the way she lived her life, she was a light in my life when I needed one.

If you have ever felt nervous about your future or a difficult "life altering decision," Dani can help you find it in yourself to step forward in faith and follow your heart.

15. THE RIGHT PATH

A Conversation with Dani Welniak-Rogers...

Everyone thought I was crazy. I turned down the opportunity to play college softball in Hawaii to play Women's Professional Football. I ended up playing slot receiver and running back for the Dallas Diamonds and we ended up winning the 2008 National Championship. I also played on the first ever women's team USA for gridiron football in Sweden. We won the first ever gold medal. I have definitely learned a lot from my experience and now as a retired professional football player and I'm a sports reporter.

I grew up playing softball since I can even remember holding a bat and a glove. High school, Travel ball... playing in college was bred into me, and for a while softball was all I could see for my future.

It was Karen Seimears that found me and talked to me about playing women's professional football, she said, "You know, this is a great option for you. It's a great opportunity and you could really be a playmaker in this league." I had to evaluate and think about giving up this big softball dream I had been pursuing for something completely different. It was a tough to think I would have to give up all that, but in the same breath, I was kind of burned out of softball at that point.

At that point, I felt like by becoming a professional athlete, especially in a "man sport, I could probably impact more people and maybe even inspire young women to pursue their dreams. I talked it over with my parents and a couple other mentors that were big influences in my life and they said, "You just got to follow your heart." In the end, I felt that God was leading me to be a Dallas Diamond. I would not be where I am today without that choice. I do not regret it in the least.

I've talked to other girls who have said "Softball is what I'm expected to do. I put so much time and so much love and blood, sweat and tears into this, I just don't see myself doing anything else or I can't see myself doing anything else." Often they're afraid to try something new because they ask, "What if I am not as good at this other thing I am interested in?" They are scared to fail. I've found when you take a leap of faith; you reach the other side, you realize your path was exactly what it was meant to be all along.

Even though you chose not to pursue collegiate softball, what role did athletics have in your growth that you have translated into your professional life so it wasn't a "waste of time"?

Any athletic experience you have helps shape the person you become! I learned how to be dedicated and loyal to teammates, how to push myself beyond what I thought I was capable of. Plus when you commit to a travel organization, you learn the time management skills you need to be successful! You make incredible relationships. You learn a lot about yourself when you learn to work with different people. You learn Things like how to consistently put effort towards your goals, every day. You get an opportunity to see your daily efforts pay off so you can reap the rewards in the long run. That is a difficult lesson for everyone and sports helps you with that!

Over 75% of youth athletes drop out by the age of 13. What would you tell a young athlete who is currently unsure if sports is worth the time and sacrifice?

I don't know you personally, so maybe playing competitive sports is not right for you. However, maybe you just need to find the right team or the right coach. What I can say is, playing sports opens so many other avenues for you. When you decide to stick to something you love and to dedicate yourself to be successful, it defines you as a person. Not only will you be successful in the sport that you're investing your time in, but it will be easier to be successful in just about every other thing you pursue. Success is a habit. Once you learn what it takes to win, it's like muscle memory; you know you have it within you!

A lot of people out there just don't know what it takes to be successful. It's amazing to me once you get to outside of the sports realm how much athletes set themselves apart because they understand the fundamentals of success. You understand the idea: I'm just going to put in a little bit of extra work into something each day, I'm going to invest in good coaching and that's going to give me an edge on my competition.

What are your goals today? How has being an athlete helped you open doors for your career?

My professional goal is to make it to NFL Network. I want to get out there and be just as good as Jenn Brown or even better. Today, I am a sports reporter and anchor in Kansas. I cover all the college football around here, which is K State, KU and then the Chiefs. I've done a ton with the Chiefs. Oh my gosh, that's been the most fun thing to cover in the world. Then we cover the Royals through the playoffs and the World Series, which was an incredible opportunity.

Remember I gave up my softball scholarship in Hawaii. I chose to go to Oklahoma State University. Stillwater, Oklahoma was a totally different world than Hawaii.. There were definitely days the thought crossed my mind "I could have been on a beach!" But I chose OSU because they had one of the first ever sports media programs that could provide me the unique opportunity to pursue my goal.

It was different than Hawaii but it gave me that opportunity to focus on what I wanted to do for my career. I was one of the few people who in that area knew how to do sports so ESPN and FOX Sports would always contact me when they wanted somebody to help them out with the game broadcasts. A lot of times, if you go to a

178

bigger college, you don't get that opportunity. I made a lot of my contacts at OSU and those relationships are a big part of how I got to where I am today at just 26 years old.

Since you're pursuing this huge goal on NFL Network, what are some of the obstacles that you're facing now?

I was one of only three girls in the sports media program at my college. Our professors stressed to us how important it was for us to know our stuff because there was an expectation that we were just a pretty face that didn't really understand sports. Sexism is still out there and it's still very prevalent especially in the news side of things.

Because I technically work for a news station, most of the people who watch are an older generation and they expect to see men tell them the sports. When a girl gets on there and says, "Hey, I won a national championship ring and a gold medal in tackle football, I know what I'm talking about." It puts a new perspective in their minds. I'm defying the odds.

I have received multiple emails from viewers asking, "What is this girl doing on air? Why is she where she is?" I've gotten multiple angry emails. One in particular I recall was from a wife of a viewer who said she didn't like that her husband was watching me on the news. She basically complained my smile was too pretty.

People will come into your life to test you. You have to learn to stick up for yourself. It's been an interesting journey to say the least, but the beautiful thing is I've had women who have broken the mold for me. It's amazing how far our society has come when it comes to women being in the sports media realm. You see Erin Andrews and you see Jenn Brown and you see all of the reporters and anchors on ESPN. This has carried over to almost every professional field.

Ultimately, be yourself. If you are comfortable in who you are, while still working toward impacting the world in a positive way, you don't need to worry about anything! You will still get negative feedback, even while you're being a positive influence on other people. As long as you prepared for it, it's much easier to, as Taylor Swift puts it, shake it off.

What other challenges did you have to overcome in order to be where you are now in your career?

The year the Dallas Diamonds went to the world championship, everybody was hyping me up saying I was going to break records. We were expecting a phenomenal season.

In the fourth game, I came up the middle and I landed kind of funny on my ankle. There were two linebackers on top of me and one rolled off of me in a funny way and I heard my ankle pop. I didn't really think anything of it because when you're playing football everything pops. I tried to stand up and my leg gave out. My fibula was broken in two places. I had to get a plate and five screws put into. The doctor told me that I wasn't coming back all season. He said there was no chance that I would be healed in time. I said, "I don't think you know who I am." I got a second opinion and the other doctor said, "It's going to hurt like heck, but it's not going to cause any damage. If you commit to intense daily rehab, you can play on it."

This injury should've taken me months and months to heal from, but I rehabbed like a crazy person and got back in six weeks. I was not a 100% but I was still back out on the field practicing when we made the playoffs. It was excruciatingly painful. Not only physically but also mentally going into rehab every single day, often feeling like there was no end in sight. Fighting the voice saying there's no way that I'm ever going to come back from this.

I had to battle with my own mind telling myself, "I can do this! If I can just overcome this pain, then you will be back. Your team will make the playoffs. Your team will go to the super bowl and you will be back for that." I had to just keep repeating that to motivate myself. And I prayed a lot. Oh my gosh. If I did not have the grace of God with me throughout those six weeks, I would not have been able to do it on my own.

Through His word, through prayer, and pure optimism, I made it back to the playing field, plate, knee brace, ankle brace and all. My coaches told me the night before during film session, they came up to me and they said, "Dani, we're going to start you in the championship."

I literally went back to my family that night and just sobbed. It was the peak of all of the hard work, and the prayers, and the blood and sweat and the tears paying off. I got to play with my team and help them win the Women's Professional Football National Championship. That was probably the toughest and most incredible journey that I had to go through and it's definitely made me who I am today.

Success doesn't just happen; it takes a lot of work. In sports, you work all those days up to just one game, just four quarters, or 7 innings. The people that watch the game have no idea what happened off the field that week. All they see is what happens for those couple hours. You just have to realize that there's so much more going on behind the scenes.

How has your relationship with your parents and mentors impacted your career path?

Prayer is a big part of my life. My parents are a huge influence in my life. As many times as I think that they're kind of ridiculous when I look back on their advice I realize they were totally right. It's the same thing with my mentors. I've had two college professors that were incredible influences and so supportive, not only helping me find a job, but they also helped groom me into the leader I am today.

What advice do you have to a young person now that has big career goals, and wants to keep playing sports and still have a social life?

I lived in a single parent household, so on top of getting good grades and playing travel sports, I had to work so I could go to college. There were a ton of times that I had to put social outings on the back burner because I wanted to be successful.

Looking back now, that's one of those things that still set me apart in today's world because I'm able to focus in on whatever I want to accomplish and what my goals are. Today, that sets me apart from a lot of people who otherwise would decide to party, or do things that will take your attention away from your goals and your dreams.

MVP leadership Academy is setting a precedent for so many young women. Not only will it help you athletically, but mentally, spiritually and emotionally as well. You get to have that community of friends, and get a great foundation for success in all areas of your life no matter what path you choose to pursue. I am so honored to be part of your power team and I can't wait to see what amazing careers you decide to pursue!

Do you have any final words of wisdom?

Never be afraid to test the waters and try something new. Remember no matter what you pursue, you're going to be met with resistance, but always pursue something and pursue it with your whole heart. Follow you heart, and know you've got the support from your mentors, from God, from friends and you're going to be successful no matter what you path you take as long as you go after it with your whole heart!

READY TO PLAY UP?

 Are you on the right path? Download the #LoyoLife Guide, and get a checklist of important deadlines for college-bound athletes so you can keep your options open!

Log in with your parents at www.LoyoBook.com/guide

Meet Coach Chez

Earlier we mentioned how your career is like the tires on your car. Here's the thing about tires; if the air pressure in the tires get to low first you won't get good gas mileage. It will cost you more to get to your destination. As the seasons and temperatures change, the air in your tires needs to be checked and sometimes refilled.

If you let the tread wears down until the tire is bare, you put yourself and your passengers in danger. Without tread you could go off the road all together. You can keep your personal tires in good shape by learning to fill yourself back up by investing in yourself. The faster you want to go towards your goals, the more you will need to invest in yourself! Chez Sievers is like Speed Racer. Any goal she sets her mind to she gets there fast because she has mastered the art of investing in herself! Her podcast Smart Softball is helping coaches and athletes learn the game of softball at a whole new level.

In this chapter, Chez shares:
- ✓ 3 easy ways you can invest in yourself
- ✓ A smile exercise to become more productive so you have more time for things you love
- ✓ How to avoid sabotaging your success

15. INVEST IN YOU

A Conversation Chez Seivers...

Softball has provided me so much opportunity in my life. I have got a ton of things going on. I just recently added to the Dallas Charge Coaching staff alongside coach Jenn McFalls. I am really excited about this journey to build a new program and be a part of expanding opportunities for athletes at the Pro level. I've assembled a team faster than I ever have in my life. I've been investing a lot of time and energy into my podcast "Smart Softball" and my efforts have opened up incredible opportunities that are great financially, and also allow me to continue to have a big impact on growing this sport that I love!

What does it mean to invest in your personal growth and what does it look like for an athlete?

Investing in your growth can mean many different things. I am only 5 feet tall and I am not growing any more physically! So the only way that I can grow is by investing my time, money and energy into learning more about the things that I am passionate or curious about. I invest in things that I feel make me a better overall person.

For an athlete, you also invest your emotions into your game. As a softball player, it's important step back and analyze your strengths and weaknesses and really devising a plan on how you can maximize the time, energy and money you invest to best athlete you can be.

I invest a lot in learning more about psychology and having a winning mindset. I don't play softball anymore, so as a coach I invest my time into connecting with other coaches that are better than me, that have been around the game longer and have more experience. We engage in conversations about how to organize a better practice or how to teach throwing, fielding, hitting in more efficient ways.

I also invest a lot in learning how to manage my time better, because I have a lot of things going on. For most athletes, this is the best place to start. Ask yourself if you are using your time correctly to maximize your growth.

If an athlete wants to know if they are making good choices on how to invest their time and energy, what can they do?

One exercise I did with my mentor was very helpful. We did a breakdown of where my time goes during the week. We wrote down things like how long does it take me to get to work? How long am I at work? How long does it take me to put together a podcast? We broke everything down so I could focus on the things that were most important to me and identify places I might be spending more time than I needed that I could cut down. Once we figured out those places I was spending too much time, we created some specific rituals.

Now, when I get ready to write a blog post, I put aside 20 minutes. I actually have a timer by my computer. That way I am reminded of how long I am working on this and really try to finish the page of writing within that timeframe. If I don't then I will take a small break and then I will go right back at it until I finish it.

It is important for you to understand where your time is being allocated. Chances are there are chunks of time where you are not utilizing it as best as it could be. You should do a check. Like checking the air pressure on your car to make sure you don't have any leaks in any area that is important to you. There are many areas that might be leaking time with out you even realizing it!

These areas might include:

Personal development: Reading, visualizing journaling, listening to audio books or training

Physical development: fitness, sports specific, and hygiene.

Relationship development: time with family, friends, professional connections or mentors.

Once you learn to identify how you are investing your time. It's important to be aware of how you invest your energy. If you are doing things that drain your energy, you are not going to have enough energy to invest in the things you really care about.

If you really feel overwhelmed with responsibility, one of the best things a young athlete can do is meditate. I really think it is important to unplug and limit the noise in your head; this helps you to practice being present, or live in the moment. This is one thing that will help you make the most of your time in everything that you do.

Can you explain in more detail what meditation is how meditating can help us reach out goals?

The best athletes and best performers in our sports are the ones that play in the moment. Most of the time, when we think about a time we failed it's because we weren't in the moment. Some people call it being in the zone or being in flow. It is important to understand how to get in that flow. The only way to get there is to practice.

There are many different typed of meditation. The goal of meditation is to clear your mind of chatter. Imagine just clearing your head, focusing on your breath and feeling completely relaxed! You don't realize how many thoughts are going through your head. These thoughts are distractions that can make you feel rushed, or stressed. You might feel like there is not enough time to get everything done or like you always need to be somewhere doing something else. is hard to move towards our goals when we can't focus our energy. It would be like trying to run to first base, second base and third base all at the same time. You end up just running in circles and making yourself tired.

Sometimes I go to yoga, that's a great form of meditation for me. I tried other kinds of meditation, like the whole sit down Indian style type pose, but I couldn't stop the chatter in my brain, so I had to do some movement with it. I have to focus on my breathing and my body movement. I always leave Yoga feeling amazing. My body feels better and my headspace fills clear. I would definitely recommend giving it a try.

If you are a young athlete curious about just meditating, just take baby steps. You don't have to be perfect, just practicing will help you to learn how to mange your energy better.

What other ways do we invest our energy that we might not think about?

Pay attention to the energy from people around you. I am a firm believer in being strategic about who you surround yourself with. Ask yourself if the people you hang out with are giving you energy or sucking away your energy?

One example might be someone who is constantly complaining or in constant lack. Nothing is ever enough for them. They might say things like "I've got to buy the newest Nikes." The people that are always saying, "I need this" about things there are not really needs can take your energy. People who are always complaining or whining can also drain your energy.

Recently, I was chatting with a friend and was telling her when I'm around a particular group of friends, I feel funnier. I don't feel that funny around people that I don't like. When I am around this one group, I feel hilarious. I want to be surrounded by people who make laugh, who make me smile and support what I do. I want friends that are good hearted who have nothing but the best intentions for those around them. If you want to be the best, then you need to surround yourself with the best. It will impact everything you do, including your career path.

Growing up as a softball player, I wasn't the biggest. The difference maker for me was who I practiced with. Every weekend I was playing with or against the best athletes in the country. That what really propelled me to play at such a high level, at the University of Texas. Surrounding yourself with good people is essential to success.

There is a famous quote that says you are the sum of the five people that you surround yourself with. So, hang out with friends that are smarter than you, more creative than you or more focused than you. Sooner or later, you will become a smarter, more creative person more focused version of yourself.

I grew up in Long Beach, California, and I didn't live in the best neighborhood. When I moved to Orange County, I was heard tons of people complaining about their financial situation. I just kept my mouth shut and kept moving on because I knew things could always be worse. I am going to be grateful for today and the people that are around me.

What is a good way for young people to think about investing money?

Growing up, no one taught me about money. I wish they had, but now I am older and just learning how to control my money better. I know money it a tool you use to grow yourself and make an impact in the world. Some people don't like to talk about money, and that is why they don't have any. You need to budget your money, just like you budget your time.

Because we have our debit cards, there is a lack of awareness of where our money is actually going. You have to make a plan for your money just like you make a plan for your time.

Think really specifically about how much money you want to make in life, how do you want to live? What kind of education would you like, what kind of house do you want to live in and in what city? Do you plan to have kids? Do you want to travel? Do you want to be able to give money to causes your care about? How much will it cost each year to live your ideal lifestyle? Then start creating a plan to meet those goals. The earlier you start thinking about these kinds of things the more time you have to compound your time, energy and money to create the league of your own lifestyle of your dreams.

What kind of things should athletes be thinking about in terms of investing money into sports?

Ask yourself why are you committed to this sport? Are you going to do whatever is necessary to make that dream a reality? If you want to play travel ball for a particular team, you may have to step back to figure out what is that going to really cost over a year? What can we do to cut back or make more money in order to fund that experience? I think it is important for parents to involve their kids in that conversation because the kids need to understand where that money comes from.

Tournaments, equipment, travel, everything has gone up in cost. As a parent I would feel better knowing that my kids are grateful for the work I put in, or the overtime that is put in to afford camp.

If you have a desire to play sports at a high level, never let money be an obstacle. When you start to really weigh out the cost and value, softball brings invaluable elements of personal growth and athletic growth.

There are ways you can be resourceful to make your dreams happen. If money is an issue or equipment is the issue, ask what you can do to be more creative about training?

I currently give lessons in Texas, I provide the girls I work with home exercises that don't really require them to buy expensive equipment. For example, I'll ask them to pour a big bag of rice into a bucket. They can build your forearm strength and finger strength but doing the

194

alphabets like in that bucket of rice. This is very inexpensive!

As a kid, if we didn't have a ball, my brothers and I would just make a paper ball and put tape over it and hit with the stick. I didn't get the five hundred dollar bat. I was an athlete. Give me any weapon and I can hit with it! That kind of resourceful mentality is really important to have in sports and it carries over into any career you pursue.

With the rise of Internet and social media there are so many great platforms for raising money Go Fund Me, Kick Starter and Indiegogo. If you have a compelling reason for why you are doing something, you can get people to invest in you and making your dreams come true.

What are other ways you could make money to make their dreams come true?

There are many ways to make money! First there is working income. This is when you exchange time for money. So you show up for a set amount of hours and get paid X amount for those hours that you worked that is working income. Working income could be working as an umpire for $25/game like Coach Jenn did in high school, or working at a department's store. There is also commission income. This is like when girl scouts sell a $3.00 box of cookies and get to keep a percentage of every box they sell.

Then there is passive income. So an example of passive income is a mobile app. Let's say you come up with a way you can make money with this app while you are sleeping. Once you have created it, you can continue to get paid for the work you did one time. In my life, I have a combination of working income, commission income and passive income. I think that is important for me. I love the interaction between the customers but I am very aware that I don't want to trade all my time for money. I only have so much time, and you do too! If we only trade time for money there is a limit on how much money we can make.

What kinds of things do you do for passive income?

I launched my first digital product last November. I gave myself a timeline to create a 30-day manual for infielders. It took me a great deal of time, and I wanted to be perfect. I filmed videos for it. I put together a progress log, the goal-setting sheet. Detailed exercises that I want the players to do for the off-season and then I launched it at the end of November. Now every time someone orders that they get access to amazing information that I just couldn't give to them any other way because of my responsibilities with ESPN, the NPF and my podcast.

Do you think it's possible for young athletes to be able to build a part time business or even create passive income?

I would definitely recommend that every young athlete gives it a try. In the beginning you just need to invest some time and energy. You will learn a lot by going for it!

There are some kids that have put together some awesome podcasts; those podcasts have led to connections with really successful people. So I would say that even if they haven't made a lot of money yet, those relationships were definitely a positive return on investment of their time!

What is return on investment?

Return on investment means you get more out than you put in. You can see a positive return on investment with time, energy or money. In terms of time, let's use school as an example. Let's say you invest 10 minutes a day working on your vocabulary words. What grade did you get as a result at the end of the week? If you normally get a C, and your studying helped you to earn an A, then you received a positive return on your time by getting two letter grades higher.

In terms of energy, let's pretend you are often tired and you even are falling asleep in class! You decided to start working out before school for just twenty minutes. After investing a little energy into this new habit for a couple weeks, you start to notice many things. You begin to crave healthier foods, you are sleeping better at night and have high energy through out the day for studying, softball practice and fun time with friends. By investing a little energy into a new habit, you see a positive return on energy in all aspects of your life.

Finally let's talk about money. One of the fastest ways to move ahead is to invest in quality coaching. Let's say you invest in a speed and strength coach. You invest $200 a month to work out with this coach a few times a week. Over three years you have invested $7,200. That might seem like a lot of money, but it was an investment in you! Imagine because you invested in a quality coach, you did not have any major injuries and your speed got you noticed by a college coach. Imagine you are offered a 50% athletic scholarship, equivalent to $11,000 per year at a public out-of-state four-year university. You were able to turn that $200 a month investment into $44,000! The return is even higher, when you consider the thousands of dollars saved in interest money you would have had to pay on a $44,000 loan. That is a positive return on investment that can change your life!

What is the biggest area that most young people should be investing in today?
Invest in things that make you feel confident. You can do this with your time, energy or your money. Invest in good books and great coaching. Invest your time and energy in doing things that build your self-esteem and make you

feel good about yourself. By investing in yourself, you will always get a positive return on investment.

Write your "Ah-Ha's" or Questions Here:

_____

_____

_____

Ready to Play Up?

 Download the #LoyoLife Guide, and get the Teen Athletes Guide to saving, making and investing money!

Log in with your parents at
www.LoyoBook.com/guide

In the next "#LoyoLife story, you will meet a young lady that isn't letting any time go to waste! Cadie invested the time we worked on a school project to change her life and helped her learn more about her future dream career.

16. JUST DARE ME

A #LOYOlife story By Cadie Hufnagle, 14

"Just dare me…" has been a common theme in my life. Both on and off the field, I have worked hard to exceed people's expectations of me. As a middle child of three sisters, I've always been "that" child. Even though, I'm the daughter of a Sheriff's Deputy and an Elementary Teacher, I've always played rough with the boys, while making my way to the front of every line.

During my sixth grade year, my mother was hospitalized in ICU for 39 days fighting for her life. She was placed into a medically induced coma, and was diagnosed with a rare, but treatable, lung disease called pulmonary hypertension. There were many times that we almost lost her, but we just kept praying that she'd be all right.

Without my mother to care for me and my sisters, our life was in chaos. Good Ol' Dad was there, but no one can replace your mother.

This taught me how quickly things can change and how not to take life for granted. My softball team was instrumental in keeping me positive and supporting me

201

through those difficult days. Watching all the doctors and nurses care for my mom and helping her through the healing process, peaked my interest in the medical field. I am happy to report that today she is doing well and continues to teach third grade.

After my mom had recovered, I had some great opportunities to play up with some older players and teams. One day I almost ruined it all when I made an idiotic decision, on a dare.

I was dared to "superman dive" over a hurdle at school. I painfully broke my clavicle (collar bone) in two places, and was luck to have not broken my neck. It was such a disappointment. I had let down my entire family, who had already packed up to support me in my final soccer tournament of the teammates that I had let them down.

I felt so guilty for not being there to support my team. During my time recovering from injury I began to see my teams fall apart. I was quickly learning that school and sports can be brutal places. I witnessed so many people morph into ugly beasts just to get ahead of their competition. The backstabbing and manipulation that can occur amongst students, players, parents, and coaches can be difficult to stomach, but with the right perspective it sure builds your character.

Seventh grade was the worst. The people I thought were my friends started teasing me for having Attention Deficit Disorder. Those were dark days for me because I had never gone through such betrayal by friends that I had trusted for years. My self-confidence was faltering a bit, but I tried to keep fighting. My sports teams became more important than ever. I was even able to use my passion for sports to help in school.

For our school science fair project I figured out a way to incorporate my passion for sports medicine. First, I investigated which wrap was the best for preventing the hyperextension of the thumb, a problem I'd dealt with on many occasions as a catcher. I was able to win third place overall in the science fair which was a great accomplishment for me since our school has nearly 600 students.

When the science fair rolled around in 8th grade I was adamant I wanted to a larger scale project to study softball injuries. I had many doubters "Cadie how can you get enough information to do a real study?" and "Cadie, that will never work, why don't you pick something a little easier. " but I wasn't going to let it go.

I came up with a great plan to do an online survey to find out what the injury rates are in Fastpitch softball and to help find ways to prevent them. This was when I found Fastpitch Fit on Facebook and met Coach Jenn!

She was so encouraging to me, and gave me ideas on how to make it all work. She suggested some questions for me to ask, and she graciously spread the word so that others would take my survey. With her help,

I was able to get over 875 surveys completed by players from the U.S. and 7 other countries, in just a few days!

My research led me to figure out that ankle injuries are the most prevalent, so lace up those high top cleats. Furthermore, I was able to share my first Youtube video to tell about my work on her site. I had so much fun doing the project, and was able to win first place at my school science fair and even went on to compete at the Regional science fair at Texas Tech University. Junior high might have started off rocky, but I sure went out with a bang thanks to my perseverance and help from Coach Jenn.

As a freshman in high school, I am still defying the odds as I continue to prove to everyone that you really can fight for your dreams and make them a reality. I was told over and over that I'd have to make a decision between athletic training, soccer, or softball. With the help of my outstanding coaches, I have been given the rare opportunity to do it all.

I was eventually able to meet Coach Jenn in person at one of her live training events. I excitedly drug both my parents with me and we are all now so grateful I did! It was truly a game changer for me because she validated the path that I was on and helped me to overcome my personal doubt. The insight that my parents learned from that one event also helped them to better support me both on and off the field.

The biggest thing that still echoes in my head today is, *"Softball is what you do, not who you are. Enjoy the journey, because it can be gone in a flash."* These are the wisest words I've learned thus far in life.

As a teenager who lives in the moment, we need to hear that softball or any sport for that matter is just a stepping-stone for what lies ahead. There is so much pressure put on us all athletes to become the star of the team, but really we should put more emphasis on the experience itself as a teaching tool to prepare us for life in general and our future careers to come.

Coach Jenn has been such an amazing blessing in my life, and I am so thankful God put her in my path. All-Star Club is changing the lives of so many and I feel very fortunate to have been given this opportunity to share my story to help others.

With her positive influence, I've continued some believed I could. So far this year, I have enjoyed marching with the award winning Soaring Pride Band, was a football athletic trainer, made the Varsity soccer my class Leo Club Representative, became a member of Future Farmers of America organization where I have served on judging teams and various leadership competitions. There have still been challenges along the way.

During one dreadful soccer practice, I got my cleat caught in the turf and tore my ACL and meniscus. Spring break surgery is now part of my history, but I have turned this devastating situation into a positive event in my life. I was secretly excited to have a first hand experience in the sports medicine field that I was so intrigued by. Going through this adventure with all my fabulous doctors, nurses, and therapists further solidified my desire to pursue my career in the medical field.

Furthermore, it has given me a chance to set back and observe other athletes and coaches in action. Reflecting back on it all, I must say that I'm stronger because of my injury. I have once again been reminded that staying positive and confident can get you through anything, and that there is always more in life than just being an athlete.

My advice to other players is to remain confident in yourself and your abilities no matter what obstacles you face. Never get down on yourself even when times are tough. Being confident is more fun and when you have fun, you can do amazing things.

I may see you on a softball field in the near future, don't let your feelings get hurt if I try to steal a base or two, or when I get you out on home plate don't take offense. I'm just doing my thing and no one can stop me on my mission. In the near future, I may even be your very own surgeon or physical therapist who may help you overcome your softball injuries. Just dare me and see what happens!

What does All-Star Health mean to you?

"Drive leads to aspirations, which leads to results and
SUCCESS on and off the field!"

Submitted by

SAVANNAH BORLAND, 15

All-Star
IMPACT
/impakt/verb

1.   have a strong effect on someone or something.

synonyms: influence, significance,
meaning;, have an effect on, make an impression
on; touch, change, alter,, transform, shape

What does it mean for you to
make an All-Star Impact ??

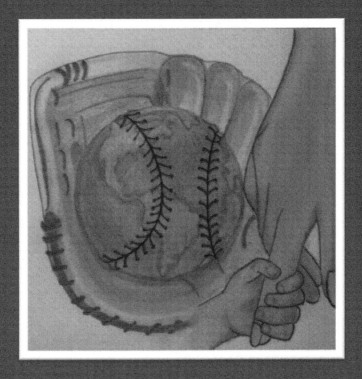

Submitted by

SABRINA OPACK-MORGAN , 16

AllStar impact means for an experienced
athlete to past on her knowledge and wisdom
to the younger generation so they can thrive
to be the best they can be."

✪ IMPACT

Impact is your ability to shine light into the world. It is why you are here. Your mission is to serve others and make the world a better place, by leveraging your unique gifts and experiences.

Impact is like the headlights on your car, shining in the darkness, leading the way for those you bring with you in your journey. Your message, the stories you choose to share with the world, the journey that you are on can be more helpful to others than you can possibly imagine. Your voice is the only voice that can tell your story the way you do.

In this chapter, you will meet two amazing leaders that are making an impact in the sport of softball around the entire world. Plus, you might get some ideas of how you can use your career as a vehicle not only to reach your personal goals but also to impact the world!

Meet Coach Joni

Let me introduce someone whose light shines so brightly it's seen all around the world!

Joni Frei is the founder of Beyond the White Lines, softball academy. She is developing champions in the game of life far beyond the white lines and beyond the borders of every country, religion and language.

In this chapter, Joni shares what you need to know about leadership in order to make the biggest impact you can in the world.

17. BEYOND THE WHITE LINES...

A Conversation Joni Frei

Every time I volunteer to be a coach or to be a leader, I always think that I'm benefiting the people that I'm working with. Ironically, it always seems that I end up receiving the biggest gift. It took 36 hours to get half way around the world to Africa.

I was asked to go to Uganda and develop their first national softball team, with the ultimate goal to bring a team to the 2016 World Championships. It's very exciting for me because it's actually being hosted in my home city at the parks I grew up in. I've committed my life to making an impact in this world by helping to grow this amazing sport. The only way this is possible for us as a TEAM is to commit to servant leadership.

Servant leadership may look different from what most people think of when they picture the word "leader." Servant leadership means we are empowering the people that surround us. It's not about getting to the top and using our followers as stepping-stones, but empowering everybody that's part of the team to be part of a bigger mission.

I haven't always operated with the understanding of servant leadership. It is something that I've had to learn and practice over time. I've realized in order for everybody to get better, myself included, it's important to empower everybody that's on the team. That is really the core of what this book and All-Star leadership is all about, Coach Jenn has empowered all of the authors to share our story with you, so we can empower you to accomplish your biggest goals. We are all on a team together.

2016 will be the first time ever that any country outside of the top 16 in the world will have an opportunity to play in a world championship. We'll have teams like Peru, possibly Kenya, Ecuador, Spain, and those countries. I would never have imagined myself being where I am even a year ago, let alone 5, 10 years ago. My commitment to serving this game just keeps opening doors.

Being a player of impact means committing to doing the right thing, not having your own selfish intentions and desires at the helm of your decision. It means doing the right thing and knowing that other people will benefit from your services. What is so special is how when you commit your life to serving others, you find you are the real winner.

If athletes learned how to be a servant leader what's 1 thing that could change in their life today? What would change in their relationships or on their teams or in school?

When you become a leader, people want to be around you. They want to be a part of what you have to offer. People want to be around someone with an empowering vision of the future. When you're positive and empowering and interested in the lives of other people, your life ends up better. It just works out that way. Your life will be fulfilled.

What's the number one thing you learned about yourself as a coach in Uganda?

I learned my standards and my expectation for excellence couldn't be compromised. It was tough. It was tough because I was thinking about how the people I was coaching didn't even eat breakfast that day. I know that they weren't drinking water because I bought the water. I bought bottles of water for the girls, so I know what they were drinking.

I had expectations, and I had to keep those standards because I knew that's what it takes to be the best. Every night, when I was done with practice, I'd go back to the hotel and ask myself; is this right? Is keeping my high expectations the right thing to do? I wasn't sure. Every day, I demanded more of the athletes I was training. Every night, I asked myself if I was asking too much of them based on their circumstances and lifestyle.

The last day I got my answer. One player came up to me and said, " We've never worked as hard in our whole life. Thank you for pushing us and making us work this hard. Thank you for showing us what we can do." If nothing else comes from Uganda, other than that comment, it was worth the entire investment for me. That is the most powerful statement because it means is that these girls didn't know what they were capable of doing, not just on the softball field, in everything. It will make new realities possible for their entire community. If you can exceed limitations and expectations on the softball field, you can do it anywhere.

Why is it okay for you to have such high expectations and standards of those around you?

It isn't my place or your place to make excuses for the people around us. If I had lowered my expectations of the athletes in Uganda, I would have stolen their potential away from them. People will meet your expectations. Most of us just don't know how great we can be. You have so much untapped power inside of you!

For the Ugandan women being able to play in a World Championship will be the biggest thing that has ever happened to them, not only in softball but also in their life. If you live a great life, if you expect greatness from yourself, if you expect excellence, then the opportunities are endless.

You never know who's watching. You don't know who's listening. You don't know who's reading. You don't know where the next opportunity is going to come. If you live great and you have high expectations, the sky is the limit. It is the #LOYOlife motto: If you want to have opportunities that only 1% of the population have, you have to be willing to do what 99% of people aren't willing to do.

I was talking to Sarah Purvis, she is one of the pro pitchers on the Dallas Charge. I used to coach her when she was a kid.

One of the things she was telling me was when she was in college. There were certain times on her team she was the one person always cheering. She was the person who was staying positive even when the team was down by 7. If you're down by 7, it's hard to find positives but she was and she was always picking her teammates up. Her teammates didn't always like that. They didn't always they liked her positivity. Sometimes they wanted get down on themselves! But look where she is now. She's the kid on a plane headed to Italy to play internationally, and she's the kid playing professionally!

That's what separates the good from the great. You always find the positive and pour that vision into the people around you.

What do you do when you hold high standards for the people around you and they don't meet them?

There was a time I was working with a coach and we didn't have the same philosophy. We had very different ideas of what our players were capable of. He was worried about working our team too hard. I knew it took hard work to be great and I wanted our team to be great!

I had two choices. I could go against his philosophies and that wasn't a good option because I didn't want to be disloyal. Loyalty is one of my personal values. The other option would be to take a back seat because he was the head coach, which would mean to lower my standards. This wasn't a goo option either because I would still not be staying true to my core beliefs and values.

Ultimately, I chose to remove myself from the situation. It was one of the toughest decisions that I have ever had to make. I could have easily been that coach that decided to do my own thing with in the organization and not cared about philosophies, but two visions equals division and that isn't healthy for any team. I wasn't the head coach, so I made my choice to leave with integrity and out of respect for loyalty. I did it the right way. It worked out in the best interest of everyone and no bridges were burned. Doing things the right way with your values in tact is not always the easy, but it is an important part in becoming a leader.

Why is it important to be a leader and live a life of Impact?
Our future is at stake. If we don't stand for something, we stand for nothing. If we don't have the ability to speak our minds, share our thoughts, someone else will take advantage and capitalize our lives for us.

What has made you the leader you are today?

The credit goes to all the people that helped me get there. There's no way I would ever have been able to do it without the coaches and the supporters that invested in me.

Why is important to grow the game?

Sport allows us to connect. For example I have never even met coach Jenn in person but she is like my sister. We understand each other, we care about each other, we live in different countries and that very real relationship developed initially because we both have a passion to grow others and help young people become successful beyond the white lines.

We are all connected through the game. Ugandans, Israelites, Jewish, Christian, Canadian, American, Chinese, Russian, Slovakia... all nations and nationalities.... cultures and religions...regardless of if our governments are at war. I have friends all over the world, and they have become my friend because of the game.

I owe all it all to the game. To the lessons that it has taught me, the expectations that it's had of me, the opportunities it has given me.

If North American athletes could go to Uganda, what would they learn?

The kids there used sugar cane bats and tennis balls, they used cardboard for bases and all shared the gloves. They had bare toes exposed, yet their SKILLS were amazing!!! I really mean that too! If we took a team of 11 year olds from anywhere in North America and a team from Uganda and let them play, Uganda would win. They're resourceful. They're appreciative. They genuinely care about each other. Those qualities make for a great team.

There is a story that is shared often that is what I experienced in Africa. The story goes like this:

An anthropologist proposed a game to the kids in an African tribe. He put a basket full of fruit near a tree and told the kids that who ever got there first won the sweet fruits. When he told them to run they all took each others hands and ran together, then sat together enjoying their treats.

When he asked them why they had run like that as one could have had all the fruits for himself they said: "UBUNTU, how can one of us be happy if all the other ones are sad?"

'UBUNTU' in the Xhosa culture means: "I am because we are. The Ugandan people play the game for the most purest, untainted reason; A simple love for the game. I saw the same in Europe when I coached and played there. They didn't play for the scholarship, the trophy, or the grandiosity of the game. They play because they simply love the game. They love their team, they love to work hard, they love being a part of something greater than what they could ever create alone. They live by the Ubuntu Philosophy- " I am who I am, because of who you are." This is the foundation of servant leadership.

READY TO PLAY UP?

 Ready to be the leader you were born to be? Download the #LoyoLife Guide, and find out how you can work with All-Star Club to make an impact in your local community!

Log in with your parents at www.LoyoBook.com/guide

Meet Coach Savana

You have now seen stories of how softball, sports and leadership can become a vehicle for you to pursue your passions and make an impact in the world. Savana Lloyd is no exception.

She's a go-getter, she's detail oriented and she has a passion for filling your heart with messages that inspire you to feel and play your best. She has been able to launch a business that has positively impacted girls in the United States but has also provided a platform to grow the game across the world!

In this chapter, Savanna will share insight on how you can discover how you want to impact the world. Her story is a beautiful example of how your many puzzle pieces can come together to give you a platform of impact!

18. INSPIRED DESIGN...

A Conversation Savana Lloyd

Softball taught me to work hard, how to stay focused, to be patient, the importance of teamwork, the art of losing gracefully, and most importantly, **you can accomplish anything you set your mind to**. I wasn't a natural athlete, but I worked hard.

By the time I got to high school, I had earned a spot playing on an internationally recognized team, traveling all over the country playing softball. Softball was now giving back to me in ways I never would have imagined. I was seeing the country, meeting amazing female athletes and playing a sport that I loved.

I earned a scholarship to play softball at Boston College and later transferred to Texas A&M. After playing I started coaching pitchers in Southern California. One of the things that I observed while coaching is how unfeminine and uncomfortable the uniforms and sports apparel are for young girls in softball. I realized there was a need for something better!

The truth is, girls have to feel good to play good. My close friend, college teammate, and ESPN Softball Analyst, Amanda Scarborough and I have spent countless days coaching together. We always have believed when you feel good about yourself, physically and mentally, you will be your best self and your best athlete. This has always been a central theme in our coaching. Amanda and I began to realize there were many limitations to the way softball apparel has been designed in the past. So we decided to create a new brand of sports apparel. Our brand, bellalete was born.

What does bellalete mean?

The name bellalete came from the Spanish word for beautiful, "bella", and the word "athlete", combined together: beautiful athlete. bellalete is a brand that not only allows girls to feel excited about their softball clothing, but also for us to use the bellalete brand, as a vehicle to help girls reach their full potential!

When bellalete first began, we started with simple t-shirts that featured inspiration words printed on them, knowing that we wanted to eventually design and manufacture our own thoughtful apparel inspired by softball girls, created for softball girls.

We knew we wanted to start with a new softball pant, however, making the leap from an idea to an actual physical product has been a difficult journey.

There have been many late nights, early mornings, many on vision boards and piles and piles of fabric samples. I would put on pairs of softball pants and my mom took chalk and just started drawing all over them with new ideas and input. February 2015 we launched our first ever bellalete softball pant!

It was a team effort. It took many people including professional designers, current softball players, and many others who support our dream and vision.

If an athlete thinks the idea of one day starting a business sounds exciting, what advice would you give to them?

First, find a need. Second, be clear on *why* you want to do it. Ask yourself, what is the need and what is the purpose? With that said, be open to change. This ability to change and to be open to new ideas is something that has really lead bellalete to where it is today. We listen to what our market is saying and move forward by building based on the feedback we get. It important to have the flexibility and adapt while also remaining true to your core values and mission.

What is your mission? Why did you decide to build a business within the sport that you played?

With bellalete, we are on a mission to create clothes that speak to girl athletes with big dreams. Softball taught me to be tenacious in my approach to life, to work hard, to chase dreams, to not take no for an answer. Growing up, I did many sports and I still do. Softball has never been "MY ONLY THING." I'm a northwest girl, born and raised in Kirkland Washington. I love anything and everything outdoors, snow skiing, water sports, hiking, climbing, cycling. Anything active and outside, I'm in! By the strong influence of my days in the dugout as a batgirl for the University of Washington, I found love and passion to be really dedicated to softball at a young age. bellalete allows me to combine my love for softball and my love for apparel, it was an easy choice!

In what ways has bellalete allowed you to give back to the game?

bellalete is allowing me to give back to the game in many ways. The ability to still be involved in the sport as both a coach and an entrepreneur after several years as a player is very special. I get to be around the up and coming girls, teaching, inspiring, sculpting and sharing lessons of both softball and of life.

This past year, I had the opportunity to coach in Europe. In preparation for my trip, I designed a t-shirt that said "Grow the Game, One softball girl at a time". I wanted to encapsulate everything that softball meant to me in a shirt for my students to wear. As I distributed these t-shirts, I started collecting stories from the many young athletes I met. It turns out this t-shirt grew into this mission called "Grow the Game."

The purpose of Grow the Game is to give back to the sport, while sharing stories. It's so amazing to think that all around the world, no matter what your background is, how old you are, we can all connect through this sport of softball, what the sport teaches us, what it does for the big picture of our lives is unbelievable.

Are there any stories that really stand out?

There is one girl we are working with right now. Her name is Lorena and she lives in Croatia. I met her while she was visiting the US on a special trip, We made a great connection and I got to hear her softball story and dreams. I asked her, "What is your biggest dream of softball? What do you want out of it?"

She said, "I want to play college softball in the US." My mind starting working on how we could make this happen for her! She connected me with the Croatian Softball Federation and I actually ended up staying with her and her family for two weeks while I did some pitching clinics there. When I saw the level of play she is surrounded with, I realized just how huge of a mountain it is for her to climb to reach this dream We had a conversation one night and she was just so passionate, she was in tears explaining to me, whatever it takes, she wants it and she won't give up.

Through Grow the Game, I've been able to help advise her towards an opportunity to play college here in the US. It's been an amazing experience for me to get to see her. She sends me Facebook messages with daily updates

This girl is dedicated. She takes different bus routes for an hour to get a field where she can practice. Some days it's snowing, and she is practicing on the ninth story deck of her family's apartment building. In Croatia, it's different because they don't have college softball. They're not used to the same work ethic in their sport. It's more just for fun after school or after work for some of them.

But Lorena is putting in the work every single day. Hours and hours of work to try and get here without even knowing if it will work out. It's still super far fetched for her to do it, but we're getting really, really close.

English is not her first language, which is interesting because every school in the US is different. We're looking to get her into a junior college, because it's a little bit easier of a transition than going straight into a four-year university for her, because where she is with her English and where she is with her skill level as far as softball.

She worked in a bakery over a month, long hours, she would go work in this bakery early in the morning and late at night for six weeks, just to be able to afford the money to pay for her entrance exam for her English proficiency. Every day this is really changing her life, teaching her how to work hard, but I think for all of us American kids it makes you really think about what are you willing to do to reach your goal? For her, there's still no telling whether or not she's going to get it.

Not only her studying for her test and putting lots of hour in there, but she is also her putting in the hours to raise the money to take it. The other thing is most of the people around her don't support her, they don't believe in her and they ask her questions like. "Why are you putting so much into this?" "Are you sure that this is something you want to do?" and "What if you don't make it?"

She's overcoming everybody around her who doubts her. She probably has more people around her doubting her than people rooting for her, but she is learning the self-discipline to tune out all of that, which is not easy. The important thing for us to ALL remember is if you put in your all, giving one hundred percent of what you have, every day... that in the end, if your goal doesn't work out exactly the way you had planned, it's going to end up leading you in a direction that will allow you find success in some other way.

I keep reminding Lorena, that no matter what happens, Your journey you are will impact your life in such a positive way, keep pushing until the very last minute. The minute you either decide to not do it or the minute that you get accepted.

Is there a time in your life where you can relate to that feeling of where Lorena is at now? When you really didn't know if something you were working so hard for would work out?

I was never a natural athlete. From a young age I had the goal to pitch in college. I had lots of people that doubted me, in fact when I first started a coach told me to pick a different sport. I worked at it every single day. I was up early and up late training, I just could not get enough. I used to take my dad into the backyard and be

229

pitching past dark. I remember jumping up and down in between pitches to get our motion sensored lights to turn on so that I could keep pitching.

I'm there right now with my business. I believe in it, and work for it everyday, but it's still a challenging, wild ride. My dad always tells me, "You're climbing a mountain. The closer you get to the top, the more difficult it becomes. Stay on course."

The better you get, or the more advanced you get, the smaller the adjustments you need to make are. The smaller adjustments are often harder to make. It also takes a lot of mental toughness because whenever you start a new journey you can see these huge strides, and it's really rewarding, because there is so much room for improvement. But as you refine your skills the more precise your adjustments must be to continue to improve. It's important to remember to celebrate even the tiny accomplishments in life.

When was your biggest struggle and how did you get through it?

It's hard for me to answer that. Of course I have big struggles, we all do. I am super optimistic, I get it from my Mom. I try not to allow challenges to make me feel low; I choose to look at the positive side in everything. If you can keep your eyes moving forward, you'll be great. If you are down, determine what triggers you to find happiness and find belief in yourself again.

What are three things that you would say to young girls that want to have a BIG impact in the world?

First, find passion for something and work hard for it. If you get really committed, it's not a matter of if your work will pay off; it's a matter of WHEN.

Second, remember that if you're not putting in the work, then there's competition out there that is. This idea can either excite you, or put fear in you. That's something I always keep in mind. I'm aware of my competition, who they are and what they're doing out there. It never keeps my from doing my thing, but it keeps me motivated to keep working hard.

Third, set plans and expectations for yourself. For me I have discipline and dedication to stay physically fit. If I go to a workout class or a crossfit class, it's really easy to work really hard because I have a coach there pushing me. If I need to do it on my own with no one watching, then I will clearly write out a workout ahead of time. Once I write it down, I know I'll get it done. If you can set the expectations ahead of time and be organized with a plan that will really help you.

There is also a fine line that should be noted, because if you are still ten and under and you are just playing softball to go out and have fun, that is GREAT! You may not need as much structure, go have fun! But the day you cross the line where you have a goal you are pursuing, that's the day you start creating a plan for how to obtain that goal. If you do this too early, just because you think you are supposed to, and not because you want to, it can take away the fun.

When I coach, I really take into consideration the personality of the girl that I'm working with. Some athletes thrive off of a programmed workout and some do not. I think it's important to know yourself and what you need to stay motivated toward your goals.

What is one thing you are most grateful for right now in your life?

I am grateful for the amazing people, mentors and the relationships that I have in my life, starting with my family, friends, pitcher parents, and all of my teammates & coaches from over the years. I have some absolutely incredible advisors. Without the people that I surround myself with on a daily basis I would not be where I am today.

What should athletes do first if they want to make an impact?

Know what inspires you. Why do you do what you do? What triggers your own self-motivation and see that, write it on your mirror. Whether it's one person, one word, or a video, understand what it is that inspires you.

For me, it is being around people that I learn from. So, I make sure on a daily basis, I put myself in front of people that I know are going to make me better. I think everyone should have something that really inspires him or her. Never lose sight of the things that keep you driven. Those are the things that will impact the world!

I'm honored to introduce you to our final #LOYOlife story of the book. I first heard Kyleigh's voice through my computer when she attended one of our free online training webinars. It's a voice, I will never forget my entire life. If you are still not sure if you have what it takes to step up and be a leader in your own life, if you still feel like you have obstacles in your way, her voice will touch your heart.

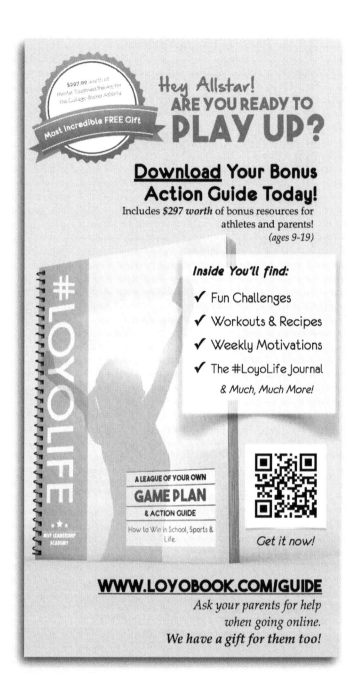
234

19. THE GIFT OF CHOICE:
Not Letting Your Circumstances Define You
A #LOYOlife story by Kyleigh Villarreal, 11

My name is Kyleigh and I am eleven years old. I have had many challenges in my life. Most of which made me feel different or out of place. Unlike my friends, I have lived with my grandparents since I was born. I have never known my mother and I have a father who is still trying to find his way in the world, which has not left a whole lot of time for me.

Looking back over the past few years, some of these circumstances have made me look at my life a little differently. I think the most challenging was overcoming the fact that I was born with a reoccurring growth on my vocal chords. This requires a minimum of at least 25 surgeries over my lifetime. So far, I have had 12 within the last 2 years.

In some ways this has made me feel like I was defective. No one could hear me and I would get very frustrated. Nothing I would say was understandable to me or to anyone else. I speak in almost a whisper.

235

It made me pull back from working towards my goals and dreams. Without having a voice, I felt like I was never heard, or taken seriously.

I was fortunate enough to get involved with sports, which taught me the importance of working together as a team. On a team, we were all working together, each one of us with different strengths and weaknesses, trying to accomplish the same task. We all made mistakes, but we soon figured out that we could learn from our failures. And in that process, our failures made our successes that much greater.

Those lessons that helped me better understand success in my personal life. Over time, I realized I have been blessed with people in my life that have come along side of me. They help me to understand that I have been given an incredible blessing; the gift of choice.

Every small thing that people have said to me to make me feel better was said with a positive and caring attitude. They saw potential in me that I sometimes could not see for myself. Those were the things that impacted me the most; guidance from coaches, mentors, teachers, family and friends.

I have been raised in a family that has taught me that our circumstances do not define us, how we handle them does. My life will always be filled with things that are out of my control. If I am not careful, I could become so focused on what I can't control that I lose sight of what I can.

By making the choice to surround myself with people that are positive and making wise decisions, I get to choose how I let the things that affect my life make an impact on me.

I have always known I was created for a purpose. My great faith has proven that to me. By learning that I can choose how my circumstances impact my life, I have discovered something about myself. I am not defective. I am made for a purpose and nothing is beyond achievement.

I have great dreams of playing college softball, and I am hopeful that one day I can play Olympic Softball. I know it takes lots of work and commitment. In fact I want to be a great pitcher like Cat Osterman, Monica Abbott or even Jennie Finch one day!

By investing my time and energy on the things that matter, instead of the things that I can't control, I can achieve great things. You can choose to let your circumstances define you as a person, or choose to make your circumstances something that will inspire you to do greater things in your life.

Recently I became involved with a program called MVP Leadership Academy. My mentor, Coach Jenn has opened doors to me that I would not have had access to. She always has a plan, she does not let me make excuses and when I am in a tough spot, she is my go to person. She and my other mentors have inspired me to work hard and focus on the things that matter.

Perhaps it starts by helping someone else through my own story, by impacting them through my own words, positive actions and making a difference just by caring about others. Most importantly, I have learned that you don't have to have a voice...to have a voice.

THE FINAL AH-HA

Part 1) Take a moment to read through all of your
"Ah-ha" moments then fill out the following questions!

NAME _____ Age_____

Before reading A League Of Your Own I was feeling...

My favorite story from this book was...

Now I feel ...

```
_____

_____
```

Part 2) Now think of three people in your life that you think should also read the messages in this book...

1 _____

2_____

3_____

Part 3) It's time to have an impact!

Call a friend today and share what you learned.

After your call, write down anything you notice about your relationship or in your emotions!

Did you get any new Ah-Ha moments after sharing?

"Being an all-star is an opportunity to inspire that little girl in the stands watching my every move, wanting to be like me when she gets older. Just as I did when I was the little girl in the stands."

Submitted by
Taylor Dorris, 14

Would you like to share your story and become a published author or artist in an upcoming book or the #LOYOLife Blog?

Take a photo of your FINAL AH-HA or Type it up
and email it to IMPACT@LOYObook.com,
or use #LOYOlife in social media.

Draw your picture below

To Me All-Star Leadership Means:

All-Star
SPIRIT

/spirit/ noun

1. **the nonphysical part of a person that is the source of emotions and character; the soul.**
   - those qualities regarded as forming the definitive or typical elements in the character of a person, nation.
   - the presence of God

synonyms: soul, psyche, innerself, truth

What does it mean for you to make an All-Star Spirit ??

"You have to be 100% dedicated to the things you are passionate about. All-Star Spirit means you are committed to the things you love and willing to practice them day and night to get better."

Submitted by

ASHLEY BALLANCE, 14

20. CAPTAIN OF THE TEAM

A message from Jenn Starkey

I first remember meeting God in the shower. I did not know it was Him. While I grew up in a Christian home, we spent our weekends and weeknights at ball games and practices, so I did not grow up in the church.

For most of my early life, I would pray with others in-group settings, but when it came time to pray on my own - I only did it when I was in big trouble, kind of like a last ditch effort. Even then, I didn't know if I was doing it right!

I think about how I would feel if my best friend only came to me when they were in big trouble, I would still love her, I would still help her, but I mean come on! It would be nice to have a relationship and celebrate together once in a while too.

I did not understand what it meant to have a relationship with God. I did not understand what it meant to hear him speak. While I didn't identify as a non-believer, I also felt kind of weird when people would say things like "God was speaking to me," or "God was calling me to do something." I had certainly never heard the big booming voice from the sky you see in movies, so these types of testimonies sounded very strange to me.

After I came home from New York, I didn't really give God much thought at all, and I felt very alone. I first met God in the shower. At the time, I called him "The genius in my shower," because I did not understand what I was experiencing. All I knew was, whenever I went into my shower, and the noise of the world went quiet, it was like I could hear a whisper inside of me. I would get vivid and beautiful visions of the things I wanted to create, to do and experience. Solutions to problems would come with ease. I would often run from the shower, wrapped in a towel, shampoo only half washed out, in hopes to take down all of the notes before the whisper went away.

Later, I heard stories from other famous authors, poets, speakers who described this same phenomenon of this whisper. The Whisper, to me, was like a jolt of Inspiration. It rarely came when I wanted it, but always came when I needed it. Eventually, I heard the words that changed my life.

The word **Inspire** means: *to move closer to God*.

As I opened up to this idea of getting closer to God, I discovered how tapping into that same source of inspiration felt easier. I could ask questions and get answers! It wasn't that God just all the sudden showed up in my life, I just finally recognized his voice. He had been there all along. God was the Puzzle Master. God was the voice of my GPS, whispering all of my desires from the very start. Patiently guiding me, from pit stop to pit stop while I went on the search for my puzzle pieces!

You can set your GPS to where you want to go, you can have a reliable vehicle to take you there, but if you are not tuned in to The Spirit, it's a long and lonely road.

The moment I surrendered to the fact I was just a small piece of the grand puzzle God designs, my personal puzzle pieces began to fit together. I discovered the perfection I had been craving so long ago. God was always in control. Your faith is the core of who you are, what you do, and who you become. Those who commit to building a lasting relationship with God will live the perfect life of impact; fueled, focused and fulfilling.

Dear All Star,

Woo-Hoo! Congratulations!

You made it! On behalf of the Legacy League, All-Star Club and Team Impact, we are so proud to be part of your Power Team! Throughout the past pages we have covered basic principles from each of the 7 Pieces of the *Play Up Puzzle*. We hope that you continue to invest in yourself so you can continue on the path to be the leader you are destined to be.

Remember to celebrate where you are today in all aspects of your life. Acknowledge yourself for being one of the 1% of the population, which not only picked up the read this book, but also made good on your commitment to finish it. There is zero doubt in my mind that you are a person of impact! I encourage you to share your stories of struggle and success; you are the one holding a piece to the puzzle that makes our world better. When you are ready to officially join MVP Leadership Academy, we will welcome you with open arms! Make sure to get your $297 worth of free bonus content today at **www.LoyoBook.com/guide**

I challenge you to Play Up!
On Your Team,

Jenn Starkey

PS: I'd like to introduce you to our final contributor to "A League Of Your Own" 3x Olympic Gold Medalist, Leah O'brien-Amico.

Leah has been part of amazing teams. While she has experienced many successes, she has also never forgotten where her light comes from. Please enjoy this bonus chapter with this amazing role model, who is truly living a life of impact.

Artwork Submitted by
Kyleigh Villarreal, 11

21. THE ARMOR OF GOD

A message from Leah O'Brien-Amico...

As a softball athlete, I practiced and prepared for whatever competition I was going to face. I wanted to do my best to be ready for whatever challenge was going to come my way. That included being physically and mentally prepared when I took the field or entered the batter's box. Even with all of that preparation, there is a uniform and equipment that I needed in my sport. When game time came, I needed to make sure I was in the team uniform. I had my cleats on my feet and a visor on my head. When I took the field, I made sure to grab my glove so I could stop any ball being hit in my direction. In the batter's box I wore my helmet for protection and my

batting gloves for a good grip on the bat.

The most important tool on offense was the bat I was swinging. I wanted the bat that I could swing with accuracy and speed and the one that would give me the most distance when I made contact.

The Bible talks about a battle that is happening all around us in the spiritual realm. It is something we can't see with our eyes at times but we can sense as we go through trials and tribulations. I am thankful that we are not to fight that battle alone. We are to be strong in God's power and we are told to put on the full armor of God. Just as we would never go up to bat without a helmet when a pitcher has a high velocity fastball, we never want to face the trials in life without putting on "God's armor."

According to the Bible, these pieces that are important for success and victory include being ready with truth, righteousness, and the gospel of peace. We are told to stand firm and when we understand who our God is and who He has made us to be with Him on our side, we know we can approach any challenge head on.

On the defensive side, we are told to take up the shield of faith. The Bible says that we do have an enemy who is trying to find ways to take us down but we must never lose our faith in God. When we are reminded that we have victory in Christ because of what He did on the cross, we can have faith that we will stand even when trials make us feel otherwise.

Finally, the helmet of salvation and the sword of the Spirit (God's Word) are how we can move forward in confidence. Those who have made Jesus Christ their Lord are promised eternal life in heaven through His sacrifice on the cross. Knowing God's Word, hiding in your heart, meditating upon it, and believing it completely are the keys to living out your purpose and overcoming every trial you face.

I have found this to be true in my life and it can be true in yours. It is when we are not "putting on" the armor that we struggle to see past our circumstances. If I start to lose my faith, live in an unrighteous way, believe lies over the truth, or don't know God's Word then I can lose sight of who I am and the victory God has promised me. That doesn't mean it's going to be easy. There is a real battle but those who will stand firm and put on the armor of God will gain ground and become leaders to those around them.

We would never enter the batter's box without a bat, so we must remember that the main offensive piece of armor is the Word of God and we should make it our priority to know what it says and to walk in that truth. When you learn to live in victory, you will become an example to those around you and they will learn that they too can experience true success with the same armor that has changed your life.

10 Finally, be strong in the Lord and in his mighty power. 11 Put on the full armor of God, so that you can take your stand against the devil's schemes. 12 For our struggle is not against flesh and blood, but against the rulers, against the authorities, against the powers of this dark world and against the spiritual forces of evil in the heavenly realms. 13 Therefore put on the full armor of God, so that when the day of evil comes, you may be able to stand your ground, and after you have done everything, to stand. 14 Stand firm then, with the belt of truth buckled around your waist, with the breastplate of righteousness in place, 15 and with your feet fitted with the readiness that comes from the gospel of peace. 16 In addition to all this, take up the shield of faith, with which you can extinguish all the flaming arrows of the evil one. 17 Take the helmet of salvation and the sword of the Spirit, which is the word of God. (Ephesians 6:10-17)

A LEAGUE *of* YOUR OWN

1. Your Personal Power Team

- A group of supportive individuals that help you to complete your puzzle
- People who live the #LOYOlife

Synonyms: The Legacy League

READY FOR MORE?

For more bonus training and up to date information on the authors in this book go to

www.LOYOBook.com/authors

The MVP Booster Club Special Thanks

The MVP Booster Club is a collection of highly regarded contributors to the MVP IMPACT FUND. Their support allows us to implement yearly Impact projects (such as this book) as well as provide scholarships to deserving applicants into the MVP IMPACT and Legacy League Programs.

With out their support this book would not be possible. You may never know them but they are certainly on your team! *Here are some words of encouragement from the MVP booster Club to you.*

Proceeds from "A League Of Your Own" go towards the MVP Impact fund.

Find out more how your business can contribute at
www.MVPleadershipAcademy.com

Special Messages from MVP Booster Club

No one has the right to cast judgment on your dreams. However, they can whole-heartedly support you in your journey. Get excited, light your hear on fire and people will drive for miles to see you burn!
- *Shauna Ekstrom & Dr. Scott Peterson*
www.HeartfeltNetworkMarketing.com

Everyone will eventually experience circumstances that challenge them in what they believe and you can either spend your time focusing on what you can't control and let it inspire you to do great things.
-Alan & Debbie Hunter,
In Memory of Jessica Hunter
www.IknowJessica.com

Your athletic career - short or long (and I wish for all of you it is as long as you desire, meaning you are in control of when you finish not external factors like injury, money, jobs, parents etc.) will be the most exciting, rewarding and enjoyable years of your life. Treasure them, enjoy the ups and downs, and always keep a smile on your face!
- **Natalie Cook**
5x Olympian, Beach Volleyball

You have unlimited potential and you can have unlimited success! - **Catherine Hall**

http://www.catherinehallunlimited.com/

You are only as good as the person next to you. Don't live your life in the middle. Stand for something or you stand for nothing. This is not about you, it always been about us.

-Dianne Baker

www.SchuttSports.com

People will believe in you to the exact degree that you believe in yourself.

-Michelle Prince, Ziglar Legacy Certified Trainer

www.MichellePrince.com

As we let our light shine, we unconsciously give other people permission to do the same. As we are liberated from our own fear, our presence actually liberates others."
A quote by Marianne Williamson

Jason Moss,

www.georgiamanufacturing.com

People will always talk and you can't stop them but it is up to you to NEVER allow their opinions to touch the core of who you know yourself to be: loving, kind, talented and a joyful human being. - **Dr. Ron & Johanna Eccles**

http://www.conquermyeverest.com/

You were born to become a winner, not only in the eyes of the people around you, but also in the eyes of the person staring back at you in the mirror every single day. Speak kind words to your mind. Become your dream!

Jolene Rickard-Lehman

http://allpointsinspect.com/

The difference between ordinary and extraordinary is that little *"EXTRA." Give a little extra in everything you do.*

- Liz Rothweiler

http://www.stlinspectors.com

Living life by patience, gut feelings, respect for others & quality preparation will help not only on the ball field, but will set up a pattern of success in school, relationships, career, & life as a whole.

Nick Burton

https://www.bluecollarparisvictorygardens.com/

"When someone shows you who they are, believe them the first time." A quote by Maya Angelou

Brett & Gina Judd MSW.

http://www.fortunesandfamilies.com/

Jenn Starkey's Power Team
Acknowledgements

Linda and Steve Bryden

Jason Starkey

The Starkey Family

Lorrena, Janel & Steph

Jon and Stan

Dick and Carol Miller

Dianne Baker

Shauna & Scott Peterson

Cindy Villarreal

Christa Tranthum

Coach Blueprint Champions

Catherine Hall

Kathryn Perry

Cathy Chapman

Teresa Hunter

Shawn Snyder

Lisa Weber

Brett & Gina Judd

Dr. Bill and Sheila Williams

Alan and Debbie Hunter

Larry & Deb Cavegnetto

Hope Stoetzer

Adrienne Umucker

Dawn Bartollini

Kason Bryden

Josh Shipp, Yayah Bakkar & TNL

Ayzsha Ervin

Jackie Ingram

Kara Troglin

Josie Ferrandino

Johnny Rob

Kristi "Pink"Hennard

Kyle & Meg Nekrash

Chelsea Martinson

The Fogarty Family

Roy Kortmann

Terri Knecht

Sarah Maxwell & Natalie Cook

Tom Kelley

Kandace Phelps

Dr. David Phelps

Jim Fortin

Jase Souder

Holly Porter

UIC Oscar Ross

Doug Corbridge

Roger & Kelly Warner

Mike & Susan Crow

Jim & Kim Herrara

The MIC community

The Tahir Family

Karen Siemears

Dr. Linda Anderson

Kasal & Media Tech 07

Megan Denny-White

Sabrina Graves

The Welborn family

Birdville HS. Coaches,

Admin & F.A.A.C.

Coach Wade Hopson

Coach Tom Mattioli

Coach Bill & Coach Margie

Larry Banks

Coach Mark Lumley

Coach Glen Moore

Brandon Marcello

Lacy-Lee Baker

Hildred Drees

Bill Edwards

Coach McElroy

Mrs. Fallis

Debra Ellis Yocum

Micheal Valentine

Danny Detrick

Robert Stovall

The Duckworth Family

Janice (Ward) Green

Mrs. Krause & Mrs. Infeldt

Kelly Dodson

Bob Anders

Matt Lisle

Indiana Pride Softball

Indiana USFA Softball

Coach Jim & Dr. Patty Cates

APE Athletics

Throwback-Athletics

Tx Fusion Softball

Tx "Dirt Devils" Softball

The FastpitchFit Family

& Founding Members Team Impact.

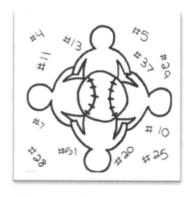

"All–Star Relationships means
having each other's backs!"
- **Abby Alonzo, 12**

"A LEAGUE OF YOUR OWN"
is the 2015 IMPACT PROJECT

MISSION. VALUES. PURPOSE.
The ultimate leadership experience
for the youth athlete.

www.MVPLeadershipAcademy.com

Book a leadership event for your
school, church, sports team or organization.

Impact@LoyoBook.com
855-808-TEAM